Aperitivo

Spritz in style with over 80 recipes for *Italian* cocktails & bar bites

RYLAND PETERS & SMALL

Designer Paul Stradling
Editor Kate Eddison
Head of Production Patricia Harrington
Creative Director Leslie Harrington
Editorial Director Julia Charles

Indexer Vanessa Bird

Published in 2025 by Ryland Peters & Small
20–21 Jockey's Fields
London WC1R 4BW
and
1452 Davis Bugg Road
Warrenton, NC 27589

www.rylandpeters.com
email: euregulations@rylandpeters.com

Recipe collection compiled by Julia Charles.
Text © Valerie Aikman-Smith, Miranda Ballard, Julia Charles, Maxine Clark, Ursula Ferrigno, Liz Franklin, Laura Gladwin, Carol Hilker, Kathy Kordalis, David T. Smith, Keli Rivers, Annie Rigg and Ryland Peters & Small 2025.
Design and photographs © Ryland Peters & Small 2025.
(See page 128 for full credits.)

ISBN: 978-1-78879-683-5

10 9 8 7 6 5 4 3 2 1

The authors' moral rights have been asserted. All rights reserved. No part of this publication may be reproduced, stored in a retrieval system or transmitted in any form or by any means, electronic, mechanical, photocopying or otherwise, without the prior permission of the publisher.

A CIP record for this book is available from the British Library. US Library of Congress Cataloging-in-Publication data has been applied for.

The authorised representative in the EEA is Authorised Rep Compliance Ltd., Ground Floor, 71 Lower Baggot Street, Dublin, D02 P593, Ireland
www.arccompliance.com

Printed and bound in China.

Notes

• Both British (Metric) and American (Imperial plus US cups) are included in these recipes for your convenience, however it is important to work with one set of measurements and not alternate between the two within a recipe.

• All spoon measurements are level unless otherwise specified.

• All eggs are medium (UK) or large (US), unless specified as large, in which case US extra-large should be used. Uncooked or partially cooked eggs should not be served to the very old, frail, young children, pregnant women or those with compromised immune systems.

• Ovens should be preheated to the specified temperatures. We recommend using an oven thermometer. If using a fan-assisted oven, adjust temperatures according to the manufacturer's instructions.

• When a recipe calls for the grated zest of citrus fruit, buy unwaxed fruit and wash well before using. If you can only find treated fruit, scrub well in warm soapy water before using.

• When a recipe calls for polenta, a fine cornmeal can be substituted if unavailable.

Contents

Introduction 7

Menu Planner 8

PART 1 *The Aperitivo Bar* 10

PART 2 *The Aperitivo Table* 48

    Cicchetti 50

    Arancini, Crocchette e Fritti 76

    Crostini, Panini e Tramazzini 96

    Pizzette e Focaccia 110

Index 126

Credits 128

Introduction

Ask any Italian, and they'll tell you that 'aperitivo' isn't the same as 'happy hour'; it's more a state of mind, and a way of being. It's a time to focus on the present moment, and process the day that has just passed, while preparing to digest the undoubtedly delicious dinner to follow.

It is also the ideal time to try a classic Italian drink. Traditionally cocktails are light on alcohol and bitter in taste, meaning they pair well with the often salty nibbles and snacks on offer. These bitter pre-dinner drinks wake up the palate and stimulate the appetite.

Campari or slightly sweeter Aperol mixed with soda are classic choices, or these can be enjoyed in a spritz or *sbagliato* with the addition of sparkling Prosecco. Try a Hugo (see page 14), a gentle and refreshing summer drink with elderflower, mint and soda. Or if you're after something with more of a kick, you won't be disappointed by Italy's most famous cocktail, the Classic Negroni (see page 26).

Delicious bite-size snacks and small plates are served alongside drinks, and depending on which part of Italy you find yourself in, these can include marinated olives, roasted nuts, slices or hunks of cheese, various *salumi* (cured meats), tangy pickles on toothpicks, small *tramazzini* (filled sandwiches), topped *bruschetta* toasts, vegetable antipasti (both cold and hot) and even freshly baked mini pizzas (*pizzette*).

Featuring over 80 delightful recipes for bar bites, cocktails and spritzes, plus suggestions for drinks and food pairings in an ingenious menu planner (see pages 8–9), this book will transport you to the bustling excitement of an Italian aperitivo hour. *Cin cin!*

Menu Planner

This planner is designed to help you put together an enjoyable and delicious aperitivo whatever the occasion. You can choose to make either or both of the suggested cocktails, and all or a selection from each recipe for food listed in the menus here. They are intended to be a guide only so feel free to mix and match throughout the book to suit your own tastes and dietary requirements.

Classic Aperitivo

The Perfect Spritz p.13

Any Bellini cocktail p.46

Tarelli p.51

Cornichons Wrapped in Salami p.63

Mozzarella Pearls Wrapped in Prosciutto p.63

Pea & Mint Crostini p.97

Salt Cod Crostini p.97

Little Fried Neapolitan Pizzas p.111

◆

Contemporary Aperitivo

Amaretto Sour p.41

Negroni Sbagliato p.18

Chilli Caramel Nuts p.52

Anchovy Twists p.58

Olive Supplì with Saffron Salt p.86

Blue Cheese Arancini & Griddled Olives p.79

Polenta Fries with Pesto p.89

Brunch Aperitivo

Prosecco Mary p.34

Sanguinello Fizz p.25

Sicilian Chickpea & Rosemary Fritters p.55

Puff Pastry Ricotta & Spinach Rolls p.94

Grilled Fig & Prosciutto Bruschetta with Rocket p.108

Italian Flatbread with Tomatoes p.118

◆

Aperi-cena (Dinner Aperitivo)

Classic Negroni p.26

High-rise Martini p.29

Fried Stuffed Olives p.60

Wild Mushroom & Parma Ham Tartlets p.75

Pecorino Arancini with Roasted Cherry Tomato Sauce p.80

Potato, Speck & Smoked Ricotta Crocchette p.84

Fresh Fig, Whipped Goat's Cheese, Ricotta & Rocket Pizza p.117

Summer picnic Aperitivo

Hugo p.14

Nonna's Garden p.14

Peppered Breadsticks p.59

Artichokes with Proscuitto p.68

White Bean & Black Olive Crostini p.102

Tuna, Black Olive, Pine Nut & Caper Crostini p.103

Tramezzini Misti p.104

Chargrilled Vegetable Rotolini p.71

◆

Fireside winter Aperitivo

Bello Marcello p.38

Sparkling Manhattan p.37

Deep Fried Sage Leaves p.57

Gorgonzola & Anchovy Crostini with Pickled Radicchio p.98

Polenta Crostini with Caramelized Fennel & Shrimp p.101

Artichokes with Taleggio Cheese & Prosciutto p.72

Thyme & Parmesan Choux Puffs p.93

Drinks party Aperitivo

Sparkling Aperitivo Punch p.45

The Negroni Cup p.42

Tarelli p.51

Anchovy Twists p.58

Peppered Breadsticks p.59

Roasted Rosemary Chickpeas p.64

Venetian Cheese with Cipolline in Agrodolce p.64

Aubergine & Tomato Toothpicks p.67

Dried Tomatoes, Fresh Anchovies & Sizzled Sage p.68

Pancetta & Fennel Puffs p.90

'Nduja & Black Olive Tapenade Mini Pizzette p.133

◆

Plant-based Aperitivo

Sunshine Negroni p.33

Strawberry Rosé Spritzer p.22

Tarelli p.51

Chilli Caramel Nuts p.52

Crispy Olive 'Pizza' p.54

Rosemary Roasted Chickpeas p.64

Pea & Mint Crostini p.91

Mini Panini Filled with 'Verdure Meditterranea Grigliate' p.107

Italian Flatbread with Tomatoes p.118

PART 1
The Aperitivo Bar

The Perfect Spritz

It is said in Venice that the spritz isn't just a drink, it's a way of life. It would be almost impossible to visit there without sitting in the sunshine sipping on one of the coral-coloured delights on offer. You can use either Aperol or Campari for a classic spritz – Aperol is slightly sweeter and less alcoholic, while Campari gives a drier result and makes a great aperitivo as the slight bitterness stimulates appetite. Recipes vary – sometimes wine is used, sometimes Prosecco. Some advocate equal quantities of Prosecco or wine to Campari or Aperol, others use a 3:2:1 ratio – three parts Prosecco or wine to two parts Campari or Aperol and one part sparkling water, but this recipe is as good a place as any to start...

200 ml/¾ cup Aperol or Campari, as preferred
600 ml/2½ cups well-chilled Prosecco or white wine
300–400 ml/1¼–1½ cups well-chilled sparkling water
orange slices, to garnish

Serves 4

Put plenty of ice cubes (never crushed ice) into four large chilled glasses and drop an orange slice into each one.

Divide the Aperol (or Campari) and chilled Prosecco (or white wine) among the glasses, then top with sparkling water. Serve at once.

Hugo

The Hugo is the Italian cousin of the classic St-Germain spritz. The addition of fresh mint leaves and lime brings bright and zesty aromas to this popular and refreshing cocktail. You can use a good quality elderflower cordial in place of the St-Germain liqueur if preferred.

40 ml/1¾ oz. St-Germain Elderflower Liqueur
5 mint leaves plus a small sprig to garnish
60 ml/2 oz. well-chilled Prosecco
60 ml/2 oz. sparkling water
4 lime wedges, to serve

Serves 1

Add ice cubes to a large wine glass. Pour in the St-Germain Elderflower Liqueur and add the mint leaves. Top up with the Prosecco and sparkling water. Stir gently to combine the ingredients, add the lime wedges and garnish with a sprig of mint.

Nonna's Garden

The gorgeous combination of cucumber and mint smells fresh and light – just like the beautiful garden an Italian nonna might spend her time tending! You can also try fresh basil or sage leaves instead of the mint, and serve alongside Deep-fried Sage Leaves (page 57).

3 large slices of cucumber, plus 1 small slice to garnish
1 teaspoon freshly squeezed lemon juice
1 teaspoon sugar
5 mint leaves
well-chilled Prosecco, to top

Serves 1

Put the cucumber, lemon juice, sugar and four of the mint leaves into a cocktail shaker and muddle well. Half-fill the shaker with ice cubes and shake vigorously. Strain into a chilled balloon glass and top with Prosecco. Garnish with a mint leaf and a slice of cucumber.

La Passeggiata

The *passeggiata* is an excellent Italian tradition of taking an evening stroll along a scenic boulevard, dressed up to the nines, to check out your neighbours. Why not give it a try in your own neighbourhood, accompanied by one of these? Serve with Cornichons with Salami (page 63), the perfect bite of salty meat and acidic pickles to accompany this bitter, fruity drink.

75 ml/3 oz. well-chilled pink grapefruit juice
20 ml/¾ oz. gin
20 ml/¾ oz. Aperol
well-chilled Prosecco, to top
strip of grapefruit zest, to garnish (optional)

Serves 1

Half-fill a collins glass with ice cubes. Add the pink grapefruit juice, gin and Aperol and stir well. Top with Prosecco and stir very briefly. If you like, squeeze a strip of grapefruit zest over the top and drop it in.

Negroni Sbagliato

No need to worry about your hand 'slipping' with the gin here – *sbagliato* means 'mistaken', and this is a rough-and-ready, but rather delicious version, of the iconic Negroni cocktail.

25 ml/1 oz. red Italian vermouth
25 ml/1 oz. Campari
75 ml/3 oz. well-chilled Prosecco

Serves 1

Fill an old-fashioned glass with ice and add the vermouth and Campari. Stir well. Add the Prosecco and stir very gently to preserve the fizz. Serve immediately.

Tiziano

This gorgeous red concoction would be just perfect to kick off an intimate meal à deux. Dubonnet's Rouge Aperitif Wine has been a staple on the cocktail scene since 1846, and rightly so!

10 red grapes
75 ml/3 oz. Dubonnet
well-chilled Prosecco, to top
strip of orange zest, to garnish

Serves 1

Put nine of the grapes into a cocktail shaker and muddle them to crush and extract the juice. Add a handful of ice cubes and the Dubonnet and shake vigorously. Strain into an old-fashioned glass, add some ice and top with Prosecco.

Squeeze the zest lengthways to spritz the essential oils in the orange peel over the drink. Garnish with it and the remaining grape on a cocktail stick.

Negroni Bianco Bergamotto

Italy is the home of the Negroni and this variation includes a few extra ingredients from the *bel paese*. The Italicus Rosolio di Bergamotto liqueur not only comes in a bottle that is itself a work of art, but it is flavoured with botanicals such as yellow rose, gentian, chamomile and bergamot orange. The sparkling Prosecco adds a bright zing and liveliness to this drink.

25 ml/1 oz. gin
25 ml/1 oz. Suze
25 ml/1 oz. Dolin Bianco
25 ml/1 oz. Italicus Rosolio di Bergamotto Liqueur
well-chilled Prosecco, to top
orange slice, to garnish

Serves 1

Add the ingredients (except the Prosecco) to a large, ice-filled wine glass and gently stir. Top with chilled Prosecco and garnish with an orange slice to serve.

Bar Note The peel of the bergamot orange used in Italicus Rosolio di Bergamotto Liqueur is most commonly associated with Earl Grey Tea, while the gentian is the key ingredient in Suze, a complex and slightly bittersweet liqueur.

Rosé Aperol Spritz

Bitter-sweet Aperol has seen a massive rise in popularity since its signature serve – the Aperol spritz – took the international bar scene by storm. This recipe peps it up further with the addition of sparkling rosé Prosecco, fragrant passion fruit juice and a hint of zesty lime.

50 ml/2 oz. Aperol
25 ml/1 oz. passion fruit juice (such as Rubicon)
1 teaspoon freshly squeezed lime juice
75 ml/3 oz. well-chilled rosé Prosecco
lime wedges, to serve

Serves 1

Fill a large balloon glass with ice cubes. Pour in the Aperol, passion fruit juice and lime juice. Stir with a barspoon and top with cold rosé Prosecco. Garnish with a couple of wedges of lime and serve at once with a straw, if you like.

Strawberry Rosé Spritzer

A gentler version of the classic Aperol spritz, this drink is deliciously light, fresh and fruity with an enticing strawberry scent. Serve as a summer aperitif alongside Pancetta & Fennel Puffs (page 90) – these savoury mouthfuls make the ideal contrast to the fruity drink..

15 ml/½ oz. strawberry syrup
50 ml/2 oz. Aperol
75 ml/3 oz. well-chilled fruity rosé wine (a Chilean Cabernet-based blend works well here)
15 ml/½ oz. freshly squeezed lemon juice
about 200 ml/¾ cup soda water
strawberries and lemon slices, to garnish

Serves 1

Pour the strawberry syrup into a highball glass or balloon glass. Add the Aperol, rosé wine and lemon juice and stir. Add plenty of ice cubes and top with soda water to taste, but no more than 200 ml/¾ cup. Garnish with sliced strawberries and lemon slices. Serve at once.

Sanguinello Fizz

This sophisticated sparkler celebrates all the sweet, tart and bitter qualities of vibrant blood oranges, and will transport you to a fragrant Sicilian orange grove in no time. For a delicious aperitivo combination, accompany it with some Puff Pastry Ricotta & Spinach Rolls (page 94).

40 ml/1¾ oz. blood orange juice
5 ml/1 teaspoon Campari
10 ml/⅓ oz. limoncello
well-chilled Prosecco or other dry sparkling wine, to top
blood orange wheel, to garnish

Serves 1

Pour the first three ingredients into an ice-filled cocktail shaker and shake well.

Strain into a chilled champagne flute and top with Prosecco. Garnish with a blood orange wheel and serve.

Classic Negroni

A perfect combination of three distinct ingredients in equal measures. When mixed, this combination is better than the sum of its parts.

25 ml/1 oz. gin
25 ml/1 oz. red vermouth
25 ml/1 oz. Campari
orange twist, to garnish

Serves 1

Add all the ingredients to an ice-filled rocks glass in the order they are listed here. Gently stir and garnish with an orange twist. Serve at once.

Note Simply upscale to batch-make Negroni – by using 250 ml/10 oz. of each ingredient, pour into a bottle using a funnel and refrigerate until ready to serve poured over ice. Ideal for parties!

Newbie Negroni

For many, the Negroni has the perfect combination of bitter and sweet complexity, but for drinkers coming across the cocktail for the first time, its intensity and bitterness can be overwhelming. This recipe has been designed to be a gentler introduction as it's served as a long spritz. The drink is both less sweet and less bitter thanks to the use of a fruit cup in place of Campari and it will work with any dry gin or even, if you prefer, a fruitier style of gin.

25 ml/1 oz. gin
25 ml/1 oz. Sacred Rosehip Cup (or Pimm's No. 1)
25 ml/1 oz. Italian red vermouth, such as
    Martini Rosso
15 ml/½ oz. orange juice
25 ml/1 oz. soda water, or more to taste
strips of lemon, lime and orange peel, to garnish

Serves 1

Add the ingredients to a large ice-filled wine glass and top with chilled soda water. If the drink is still too strong, add more soda water. Garnish with lemon, lime and orange peels to serve.

High-rise Martini

Martinis are often short and potent, but on a hot summer's day it can be nice to have the taste of a martini in a spritz-style drink that is more refreshing and thirst-quenching. Here is it served with a classic Italian small bite, Mozzarella Pearls Wrapped in Prosciutto (page 63).

30 ml/1 oz. gin or vodka
1 barspoon dry vermouth
1 barspoon Bianco Vermouth
100 ml/3¼ oz. sparkling water or sparkling lemonade
strips of lemon, lime and orange peel, to garnish

Serves 1

Add the alcohols to an ice-filled highball glass (spirit first) and give the drink a gentle stir. Top with sparkling water or lemonade and garnish with strips of lemon, lime and orange peel.

Prosecco Iced Tea

Tea, gin and Prosecco: all your favourite refreshments in one glass! Next time you fancy a Long Island Iced Tea, think again, and try this far more elegant concoction instead.

1 Earl Grey teabag
1 tablespoon sugar
25 ml/1 oz. gin
1 teaspoon freshly squeezed lemon juice
dash of elderflower cordial
well-chilled Prosecco, to top
lemon slices, to garnish

Serves 1

First, make an infusion by putting the teabag and sugar in a mug and pouring over 75 ml/3 oz. boiling water, then leave for 5 minutes. Remove the teabag and leave the infusion to cool to room temperature.

Pour the Earl Grey infusion into a collins glass and add the gin, lemon juice and elderflower cordial. Half-fill with ice cubes and stir well. Top with Prosecco and garnish with a couple of lemon slices, and a straw if you like.

Sunshine Negroni

This drink, the Negroni's answer to a Tequila Sunrise, is just as visually stunning as the original.

25 ml/1 oz. citrus-forward gin, such as Gordon's Sicilian Lemon Gin
25 ml/1 oz. Aperol
25 ml/1 oz. Dolin Bianco
10 ml/⅓ oz. orange juice
35 ml/1½ oz. grapefruit soda
5 ml/1 teaspoon grenadine
orange slices, to garnish

Serves 1

Add the gin, Aperol, vermouth and orange juice to an ice-filled highball glass and gently stir. Top with the chilled grapefruit soda and slowly pour the grenadine down the inside of the glass. Garnish with orange slices to serve.

Bar Note Any grapefruit soda can be used here, even something like Lilt, but for the optimal visual effect it's best to use a white grapefruit soda such as Ting or San Pellegrino over a ruby or red grapefruit variety.

Tintoretto

The pomegranate spiked Tintoretto is a pretty and delicious cocktail from the legendary Venetian institution Caffè Florian in St. Mark's Square. Pictured on page 1.

140 ml/½ cup pomegranate juice
600 ml/2½ cups Prosecco

Serves 4

Pour the pomegranate juice into four chilled champagne flutes, then top with chilled Prosecco. Serve at once.

Prosecco Mary

Think of this Prosecco Mary as the traditional Bloody Mary's younger, more contemporary and slightly more glamorous and 'spritzy' sister! The ideal drink for a brunch aperitivo.

25 ml/1 oz. vodka
75 ml/3 oz. tomato juice
dash of Tabasco or sriracha sauce
pinch of sugar
dash of smoked water (optional; available in some supermarkets)
about 75 ml/3 oz. well-chilled Prosecco
cucumber slices and/or a celery stick/rib, to garnish

Serves 1

Put the vodka, tomato juice, Tabasco, sugar and smoked water, if using, into a cocktail shaker half-filled with ice cubes. Shake vigorously and pour, ice cubes and all, into a chilled collins glass. Add half the Prosecco and stir gently to combine. Top with the rest of the Prosecco, add some cucumber slices down the side of the glass (or a celery stick/rib if you prefer) and serve with a stirrer.

Bar Note Smoked water is delicious but can overpower, so exercise caution and use no more than ¼ teaspoon to begin with.

Sparkling Manhattan

If you love Manhattans but sometimes find them a bit much, you'll love this. This is based on a Sweet Manhattan, but feel free to switch the sweet vermouth for dry if you prefer yours dry – or use half sweet and half dry vermouth if you're more of a Perfect Manhattan fan.

15 ml/½ oz. bourbon
10 ml/⅓ oz. Italian sweet red vermouth
dash of Angostura bitters
5 ml/1 teaspoon Maraschino, such as Luxardo (optional)
well-chilled Champagne or other dry sparkling wine, to top
maraschino cherries, to garnish

Serves 1

Pour the first four ingredients into an ice-filled cocktail shaker and stir well. Strain into a chilled old-fashioned glass and top with Champagne. Garnish with maraschino cherries.

Americano

The Americano was first served in the 1860s at Gaspare Campari's bar in Milan. The drink, which features Campari and sweet vermouth in equal parts topped with sparkling water, was popular among American tourists, which it's believed is where its name stems from.

35 ml/1½ oz. Campari
35 ml/1½ oz. sweet vermouth
well-chilled soda water, to top
orange twist, to garnish

Serves 1

Fill a highball glass with ice, then add the Campari and sweet vermouth. Top with the chilled soda water and stir gently to mix. Garnish with an orange twist and serve at once.

Bello Marcello

Even the most committed whisky-phobe will love this citrusy sipper. Surely there's no better use for that dusty bottle at the back of the drinks cabinet!

35 ml/1½ oz. whisky
15 ml/½ oz. Cointreau
well-chilled Prosecco, to top
strip of lemon zest, to garnish

Serves 1

Pour the whisky and Cointreau into an old-fashioned glass filled with ice. Stir well, then top with Prosecco.

Squeeze the lemon zest in half lengthways over the drink so that the essential oils in the skin spritz over it, then add the zest to the drink and serve.

Prima Donna

Simply combine a zesty Italian lemon liqueur with vodka, tangy pomegranate juice and chilled Italian sparkling wine, for an elegant and pretty aperitivo drink.

25 ml/1 oz. vodka
15 ml/½ oz. limoncello
25 ml/1 oz. pomegranate juice
chilled Prosecco, to top
pomegranate seeds and orange slices,
**   to garnish (optional)**

Serves 1

Put the vodka, limoncello and pomegranate juice in a cocktail shaker and add a handful of ice cubes. Shake sharply and strain into an ice-filled rocks glass or tumbler. Top with Prosecco, garnish with pomegranate seeds and orange slices (if using) and serve.

Amaretto Sour

The marzipan flavour notes from the amaretto are balanced by the zingy lemon juice and bitters in this famous cocktail. Pictured on page 78.

50 ml/2 oz. amaretto
25 ml/1 oz. lemon juice
5 ml/1 teaspoon syrup from a jar of maraschino
**   cherries, plus cherries from the jar to garnish**
1 tablespoon aquafaba (brine from a can of
**   chickpeas)**
dash of angostura bitters
dash of bourbon

Serves 1

Half-fill a cocktail shaker with ice cubes and add all the ingredients. Shake really well until the outside of the shaker is cold. Strain the cocktail into a glass. Skewer a few maraschino cherries onto a cocktail skewer and use this to garnish the glass.

Porch-drinking Negroni

This laidback drink was just made for sipping on warm summer evenings. The muddled strawberries give it a soft, fruity note while the bitter lemon adds a refreshing crispness. You can use a soft, sippable gin, or something more intense and piney, as preferred.

3 strawberries
15 ml/½ oz. gin, your choice of style
10 ml/⅓ oz. Campari
10 ml/⅓ oz. bianco vermouth
150 ml/⅔ cup bitter lemon
mint sprig, to garnish

Serves 1

Muddle or crush the strawberries in the bottom of a rocks glass, then add the other ingredients and gently stir. Add ice and garnish with a mint sprig to serve.

The Negroni Cup

A longer version of the Porch-drinking Negroni (left), this can be served by the pitcher so is ideal for gatherings.

75 ml/3 oz. gin
25 ml/1 oz. sweet red vermouth
25 ml/1 oz. ginger wine
25 ml/1 oz. Campari
450 ml/scant 2 cups well-chilled sparkling lemonade
lemon wheels and cucumber slices, to garnish

Serves 4

Combine the ingredients (except the lemonade) in a large jug/pitcher with ice and stir before garnishing with lemon wheels and cucumber slices. Top with chilled lemonade and pour into ice-filled tumblers to serve.

Sparkling Aperitivo Punch

The scent of thyme in this punch will transport you to a village nestled on a hilltop in Tuscany. This recipe makes an extra-large quantity so it is ideal for an al-fresco party. You'll need a 3.5 litre/scant 4 quart capacity punch bowl or drinks dispenser to serve. For the accompanying nibbles? Try Tarelli (page 51).

4 thyme sprigs, plus extra to garnish
1 x 750-ml/25-oz. bottle well-chilled Aperol
1 x 750-ml/25-oz. bottle well-chilled dry white vermouth (Lillet works well here)
1 litre/4 cups fresh pink or white grapefruit juice
1 x 750-ml/25-oz. bottle well-chilled juicy, sparkling rosé wine (a Cava rosada or rosé Prosecco both work well here)
pink grapefruit slices, to garnish

Serves 20

Combine the thyme sprigs, Aperol, vermouth and grapefruit juice in a jug/pitcher and chill for at least 2 hours.

Pour into a large punch bowl, add the sparkling rosé and plenty of ice cubes. Add a few ice cubes and a slice of grapefruit to each serving glass (small wine glasses or tumblers can be used). Pour in the punch and add a sprig of fresh thyme to each serving to garnish. Serve at once.

Bellini

Perhaps the most famous of all Venetian cocktails, the Bellini was invented by Giuseppe Cipriani at the celebrated Harry's Bar in Venice around 70 years ago. It's a mixture of fresh white peach juice and Prosecco. To stay true to the original flavour (and enjoy the best cocktail), only white peaches (not yellow) will do. And absolutely no canned peaches! Please! The secret is to adapt your Bellini to the changing seasons – better to try a different fruit entirely than to make a poor cocktail using under-ripe fruit, pasteurized fruit juices or anything from a can. Keep the ingredients and glasses as cold as possible. The Harry's Bar formula is about three to four parts Prosecco to one part peach purée. Why change the stuff that legends are made of? Cin! Cin!

Classic Bellini

40 ml/3 tablespoons freshly made white peach purée
480 ml/2 cups Prosecco

Serves 4

Pour the peach purée into chilled champagne flutes. Pour in the Prosecco and stir gently.

Serve immediately.

Strawberry & Basil Bellini

5 ripe strawberries
1 teaspoon white sugar
small handful of fresh basil leaves
120 ml/½ cup Prosecco

Serves 1

Whizz the strawberries and sugar together in a blender to make a purée. Pour the purée into a jug/pitcher, add a little of the Prosecco and the basil. Bash with a blunt object until the flavour has been released.

Pour the mixture through a strainer into a chilled champagne flute. Pour over the remaining Prosecco and stir gently.

Serve immediately.

Pear Bellini

200 ml/¾ cup pear purée
480 ml/2 cups Prosecco

Serves 4

Pour the pear purée into chilled champagne flutes. Pour in the Prosecco and stir gently.

Serve immediately.

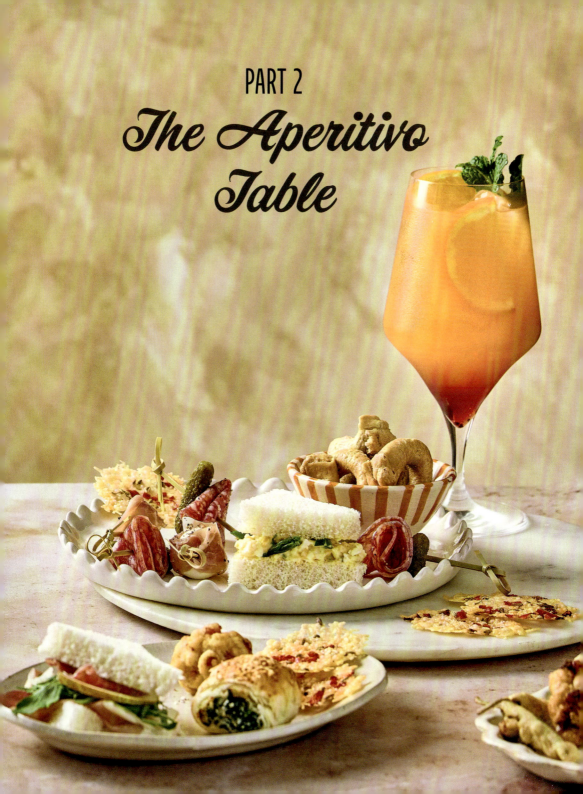

Cicchetti

Tarelli

These crunchy little savoury biscuits hail from Puglia and are very addictive. In Italy they are a classic served with aperitivo, but they are also excellent picnic snacks. In Puglia these are available everywhere, but homemade ones are unparalleled. Try adding fennel seeds as they work very well too.

150 g /1 cup plus 3 tablespoons Italian '00' flour, plus extra for sprinkling and kneading

40 g/⅓ cup semolina (fine)

1 teaspoon freshly ground black pepper or 2 teaspoons lightly crushed fennel seeds

2 teaspoons fine sea salt

70 ml/⅓ cup dry white wine

70 ml/⅓ cup extra virgin olive oil, an Italian one from Puglia if possible

2 baking sheets, oiled

Makes 30

Put the flour, semolina, pepper (or fennel seeds, if preferred) and half the salt in a large bowl. Add the wine and oil and mix to combine. Turn out onto a floured surface and knead for about 2 minutes until the dough is smooth and elastic. Place the dough in a lightly oiled bowl, cover with a clean kitchen towel and leave to relax for 45 minutes to 1 hour.

Halve the relaxed dough and cut each half into 10 pieces. Keep the remaining dough covered as you work to stop it drying out. Roll one piece of dough into a 50-cm/10-inch rope. Cut the rope into 5 pieces, then roll each piece into 10-cm/4-inch ropes. Connect the ends to form an overlapping ring. Continue with the remaining dough, keeping the rings covered too, as you make them.

Preheat the oven to 180°C (350°F) Gas 5.

Bring 900 ml/scant 4 cups water to the boil in a large saucepan and add the remaining salt.

Add the rings to the saucepan of boiling water in batches and cook for about 3 minutes until they float. Use a slotted spoon to transfer them to the prepared baking sheets.

Bake in the preheated oven for about 30 minutes until golden and crisp. Let cool on wire racks before serving.

Parmesan Fritters

This quick snack made from leftover pizza dough is often served in bars for aperitivo. All you need is some fresh Parmesan cheese and you've got a delicious appetite-whetter. Just don't eat too many!

½ recipe Basic Pizza Dough
   (page 110), making just 1 ball of dough
plain/all-purpose flour, for dusting
50 g/⅔ cup grated Parmesan, plus extra to finish
vegetable or olive oil, for deep-frying

round cookie cutter (optional)

Makes about 16

Uncover the dough, punch out the air and roll or pull as thinly as you can, flouring the surface well. Using an upturned glass or a cookie cutter, stamp out as many circles as you can – you can make them any size. Place a little mound of Parmesan in the centre of each one and fold in half, pinching the edges together.

Heat the oil in the wok or deep fryer to 190°C (375°F), or until a piece of stale bread, dropped in the oil, sizzles and turns golden in a few seconds.

Fry the fritters in batches until puffed and golden on both sides. Drain well on paper towels, then toss the fritters in some extra grated Parmesan. Serve hot.

Chilli Caramel Nuts

These crunchy, savoury-sweet chilli/chili-spiked nuts are seriously special. Perfect served with drinks for aperitivo when friends come over, but they're great to munch on whilst watching a movie too.

200 g/scant 2 cups mixed nuts (whole almonds,
   pecans, cashews, pistachios)
2 tablespoons olive oil
2 tablespoons brown rice syrup
1 tablespoon maple syrup
1 generous teaspoon mild paprika
1 teaspoon dried chilli flakes/hot red pepper flakes
sea salt

Serves 2–4

Put the mixed nuts into a large bowl. Add the olive oil, brown rice syrup, maple syrup and paprika. Stir in the chilli/red pepper flakes and a sprinkling of salt. Bake for 10 minutes, stirring a couple of times as they cook.

Leave to cool – and try not to eat them all before serving with drinks.

Crispy Olive Flatbread

Schiacciata is a dialect word meaning 'flattened,' so some Italian flatbreads, such as this one, are known as *schiacciata*. This recipe uses olives and leftover pizza dough to create a simple bread that is perfect for dipping into extra virgin olive oil.

½ **recipe Basic Pizza Dough**
(page 110), making just 1 ball
of dough
splash of white wine
handful of green olives, stoned/pitted
and roughly chopped
coarse sea salt
extra virgin olive oil, to serve

a testo, terracotta baking stone or
a large, heavy baking sheet
a large rimless baking sheet

Makes 8–12

Put the testo, terracotta bakestone or a large, heavy baking sheet on the lower shelf of the oven. Preheat the oven to 220°C (425°F) Gas 7 for at least 30 minutes.

Using a rolling pin, roll the dough out as thinly as you can, directly onto the rimless baking sheet. Brush the dough with a little white wine, scatter with the olives and sprinkle with salt. Lightly press the olives and salt into the dough. Using a pizza wheel, score the dough in lozenge shapes directly on the baking sheet.

Bake for 5–10 minutes until the bread is puffed and pale golden. Remove from the oven and break up into the pre-cut lozenges.

Serve warm with olive oil for dipping.

Chickpea & Rosemary Fritters

Versions of these versatile little fritters are popular throughout the Mediterranean, especially in Sicily, where they are eaten as street food and known as *panelle*. The fritters are crisp on the outside and soft in the middle. To taste their best they must be served hot and sprinkled with lots of sea salt – the perfect accompaniment to a pre-dinner spritz on a sunny evening.

300 g/2½ cups chickpea (gram) flour
1–2 tablespoons chopped fresh
**   rosemary**
vegetable oil, for oiling and
**   deep-frying**
sea salt and freshly ground
**   black pepper**

Makes about 40

Lightly oil a cold surface such as a marble slab or the back of a large baking sheet. Have a spatula at the ready!

Sift the chickpea flour into a saucepan. Slowly whisk in 750 ml/3 cups water, making sure there are no lumps. Stir in the rosemary and salt and pepper to taste. Bring to the boil, beating all the time, until the mixture really thickens and leaves the side of the pan (like choux pastry). Don't worry if you get lumps at this stage, they will disappear when you fry the fritters.

Now you need to work really quickly. Tip the mixture onto the oiled surface and spread it out as thinly and evenly as you can – aim to make it about 3 mm/⅛ inch thick. Let cool and set.

When set, cut into small triangles or squares. To prevent them drying out, place them between layers of plastic kitchen wrap until ready to cook.

Heat the oil in the wok or deep fryer to 190°C (375°F), or until a piece of the mixture, dropped in the oil, sizzles and turns golden in a few seconds.

Deep-fry a few fritters at a time, turning when golden brown. Drain on paper towels and sprinkle with salt. Serve hot.

Deep-fried Sage Leaves

A wonderful explosion of the flavours of sage and anchovy through crisp batter. These must be served virtually straight out of the pan. A packet of Japanese tempura batter can be used instead of making your own, if preferred.

24 large sage leaves
1 teaspoon salted capers, rinsed
1 tablespoon anchovy paste
vegetable oil, for deep-frying

FOR THE BATTER
1 egg
150 ml/⅔ cup iced water
125 g/scant 1 cup plain/all-purpose flour

Makes 12

Wash and dry the sage leaves. Mash the capers with the anchovy paste and spread the mixture onto the darker green sides of 12 of the leaves. Press another leaf on top of the filling to form a sandwich.

To make the batter, lightly whisk the egg and the iced water together. Add the flour and whisk again, leaving the mixture a bit lumpy. Do not allow to stand.

Heat the oil in the wok or deep fryer to 190°C (375°F), or until a piece of bread, dropped in the oil, sizzles and turns golden in a few seconds.

Holding the leaves by the stem, dip them into the batter and lightly shake off the excess. Place into the hot oil, a few at a time, and fry until crisp and barely golden. This will take only a few seconds. Drain on paper towels and serve immediately.

Parmesan Crisps

You'll never make enough of these thin, crunchy savoury crisps – the secret is not to cook them for too long. They are sometimes made in a frying pan/skillet, but it is much easier to bake them in quantity in the oven. They keep well in an airtight container. You can also use Grana Padano for this – it is cheaper than Parmesan and works just as well.

125 g/1⅔ cups grated Parmesan or Grana Padano
a few fennel seeds (optional)
1 red chilli/chile, deseeded and finely chopped (optional)

baking sheet, lined

Serves 4

Preheat the oven to 200°C (400°F) Gas 6.

Spoon small mounds of grated cheese onto the lined baking sheet at regular intervals. Flatten with the back of the spoon. Sprinkle a few fennel seeds or some chopped red chilli/chile on top, if you like.

Bake for 3–6 minutes until golden, then remove from the oven and leave for a couple of minutes to set. You can curl them over a wooden spoon handle or rolling pin at this stage to give a more interesting shape, if you like.

Carefully lift them off the paper and let cool completely on a wire rack.

These crisps will keep for up to 4 days if stored in an airtight container.

Anchovy Twists

For all you anchovy-lovers out there, these fit the bill. Transform leftover pizza dough (or use fresh dough) by flavouring it with anchovies. The combination of these simple anchovy twists and a glass of chilled white wine truly transports you to a sunny terrace in Italy.

½ **recipe Basic Pizza Dough (page 110), making just 1 ball of dough**
50 g/1¾ oz. canned anchovies in oil, drained and chopped
vegetable or olive oil, for deep-frying
sea salt

Makes 15–20

Uncover the dough, punch out the air and knead in the anchovies. Roll or pull it out thinly, then cut into long rectangles with a crinkled pastry wheel or a sharp knife. Make a slash in the middle of each rectangle, bring one end up and push through the slit, pulling it through loosely to make a roughly twisted shape.

Heat the oil in the wok or deep fryer to 190°C (375°F), or until a piece of bread, dropped in the oil, sizzles and turns golden in a few seconds.

Fry the twists in batches until golden and crisp. Drain well on paper towels, then sprinkle with salt. Serve warm, or store in an airtight container and reheat them for a couple of minutes in a warm oven to serve.

Peppered Breadsticks

We all know the paper packets containing a couple of breadsticks which many Italian restaurants serve, but these are a more sophisticated version and can be made using leftover pizza dough. Just knead in the black pepper or any other flavouring that suits your fancy.

½ recipe Basic Pizza Dough (page 110), making just 1 ball of dough
2 tablespoons cracked black pepper
2 tablespoons extra virgin olive oil
25 g/2 tablespoons butter, melted
plain/all-purpose flour, for dusting

Makes about 20

Make the pizza dough according to the recipe on page 110, adding the cracked pepper to the ingredients.

Mix the olive oil and melted butter together and set aside.

Before the first rising, roll or pull the dough into a thin rectangle, brush all over with the olive oil and butter mixture and roll up loosely like a Swiss roll/jelly roll. Flatten with the palm of your hand, then lift it onto a floured work surface, cover with clingfilm/plastic wrap and let rise for 30 minutes.

Preheat the oven to 200°C (400°F) Gas 6.

Flatten the risen dough with your hand again to knock out the air then roll out to a thickness of 5 mm/¼ inch.

Cut into long, thin strips and twist. Lay these onto a baking sheet and mist with water. Bake for 5 minutes, mist again, then bake for a further 10–15 minutes until golden and crisp. Keep an eye on them while they are baking as they can burn.

Fried Stuffed Olives

Fried stuffed olives are often filled with a meat mixture that is based on the classic recipe for olives all'Ascolana (Ascolana is a region in central Italy that produces superb jumbo-size green olives with a mild flavour). Choosing a mild olive is really important – anything too astringent will spoil the balance of flavours. Here, we have for a lovely tomato-rich filling, softened with some ground almonds and dotted with salty speck, the wonderful cured ham from the Alto Adige region, just north of Venice.

3–4 tablespoons extra virgin olive oil
1 white onion, finely chopped
2 garlic cloves, finely chopped
400 g/14 oz. ripe cherry tomatoes,
  roughly chopped
100 ml/⅓ cup plus 1 tablespoon white
  wine
1 teaspoon white sugar
small handful of torn fresh basil
50 g/½ cup ground almonds
50 g/½ cup roughly chopped speck
30 jumbo-size mild green olives,
  pitted/stoned
3 tablespoons plain/all-purpose flour
120 g/3 cups panko breadcrumbs
sea salt and freshly ground black
  pepper
vegetable oil, for deep-frying

FOR THE PASTELLA
2 egg whites
60 ml/¼ cup sparkling water
60 g/½ cup self-raising/rising flour

piping/pastry bag fitted with a large
  nozzle/tip

Makes 30

Heat the extra virgin olive oil in a large frying pan/skillet over low–medium heat and cook the onion and garlic for about 15 minutes until softened but not coloured.

Add the cherry tomatoes and the wine. Stir in the sugar, season with salt and black pepper, and let the mixture bubble gently for about 20 minutes.

Add the torn basil, and leave to bubble for 10 minutes or so until the sauce is thick and sticky. If it looks a little too dry, don't be afraid to add a splash of water. Remove from the heat, stir in the ground almonds and leave to cool.

When the mixture is cold, stir in the chopped speck.

Put the mixture into a piping/pastry bag fitted with a large nozzle/tip and pipe the filling into the centre of each pitted/stoned olive.

For the pastella, beat the egg whites until light, then stir in the sparkling water. Slowly add the self-raising/rising flour and mix until smooth.

Roll the stuffed olives in the plain/all-purpose flour, dip them into the pastella and then coat in the panko breadcrumbs.

Heat the oil in the wok or deep fryer to 190°C (375°F), or until a piece of bread, dropped in the oil, sizzles and turns golden in a few seconds.

Fry the olives for 2–3 minutes until crisp and golden.

Drain on paper towels and serve immediately.

Cornichons with Salami

As simple as the name suggests. These mini gherkins are often served with salami because the flavours complement each other perfectly. This combination really is a delight for the tastebuds – saltiness from the meat and acidity of the pickled cornichons. If you like, you can wrap the cornichons in the salami and then skewer them, creating the perfect mouthful.

12 slices salami
12 cornichons (or 12 small slices
   of pickled gherkin)
freshly ground black pepper

cocktail sticks/toothpicks

Makes 12

For each bite, fold a slice of salami and pop it onto a cocktail stick/toothpick, followed by a cornichon. Repeat to make 12 bites in total.

Crack a little pepper over the plate and serve with drinks of your choice.

Mozzarella Pearls Wrapped in Prosciutto

So easy, just like the recipe to the left. Don't use a whole slice of prosciutto per mini mozzarella pearl/ball, as that's a heavy mouthful, as well as being expensive for entertaining. Use kitchen scissors to cut each slice of prosciutto into quarters.

3 slices prosciutto
12 mini mozzarella pearls/balls
freshly ground black pepper

cocktail sticks/toothpicks

Makes 12

Cut each slice of prosciutto lengthways in quarters (kitchen scissors are best for doing this) to make 12 strips in total. Wrap each strip around a mini mozzarella pearl/ball.

Pop a cocktail stick/toothpick through the middle of each assembled bite to hold it together, crack a little black pepper over the plate and serve.

Rosemary Roasted Chickpeas

Dry-roasting chickpeas gives them a nice crunchy texture and transforms them into a tasty, yet healthy snack, the perfect nibble to accompany drinks. They take an hour to dry out though, so you could put them in the oven while cooking something else to make the best use of the oven.

2 x 400-g/14-oz. cans chickpeas, drained
1 tablespoon extra virgin olive oil
1 tablespoon chopped fresh rosemary
sea salt flakes

Serves 8–10

Preheat the oven to 170°C (325°F) Gas 3.

Spread the chickpeas in a single layer in a roasting dish or baking pan. Without adding anything, simply leave them in the preheated oven for an hour or so until they are very dried out and crunchy. If you cut down the time, they'll just end up slightly crisp on the outside and still soft in the centre, and nowhere near as delicious. Be patient!

When they are crunchy, remove the chickpeas from the oven, toss in the oil and rosemary, and season with sea salt flakes.

Enjoy immediately or store in airtight container for up to 1 week.

Venetian Cheese with Sweet & Sour Onions

Cipolle or *cipolline borettane* are small, saucer-shaped onions that come in jars in *agrodolce*, a sweetened vinegar that makes them incredibly addictive. Asiago is the cheese you will probably get paired with your *cipolline* in Venice, but feel free to substitute your own favourite. Don't be tempted to use ordinary pickled onions though, or, heaven forbid, the humble silverskin... they're just not the same!

500 g/1 lb. 2 oz. Asiago (or other mild Italian cheese), cut into small triangles
2 x 225-g/8-oz. jars cipolline in agrodolce (pickled onions in sweet and sour brine), drained

Serves 8–10

Top the cheese triangles with the *cipolline* and secure with a cocktail stick/toothpick.

Serve on a platter with drinks.

Aubergine & Tomato Toothpicks

This simple recipe is a perfect example of a Venetian *cicchetto*. *Cicchetti* are traditional snacks served alongside drinks in Venice's *bacari* bars. Baby aubergines/eggplant are perfect for this, and look so pretty – but if you can't get hold of them, simply choose one that is longer rather than very round.

10 baby aubergines/eggplant (or 1 long, thin aubergine/eggplant)
3 tablespoons extra virgin olive oil
1 tablespoon fresh thyme leaves
2 tablespoons finely grated Parmesan
20 bocconcini (small mozzarella pearls/balls)
freshly ground black pepper
sea salt and freshly ground black pepper

FOR THE TOMATO SAUCE
3–4 tablespoons extra virgin olive oil
1 white onion, finely chopped
2 garlic cloves, finely chopped
400 g/14 oz. ripe cherry tomatoes, halved
100 ml/⅓ cup plus 1 tablespoon white wine
1 teaspoon white sugar
small handful of torn fresh basil

Makes 20

Preheat the oven to 190°C (375°F) Gas 5.

If you are using baby aubergines/eggplant, simply cut them in half. If you are using a large aubergine/eggplant, cut it in half lengthways, then into wedges that create small 'boats'. You will have to cut a little from the top of each wedge to create a flat surface. Score the surface without the skin of each with a criss-cross pattern.

Brush the aubergine/eggplant with extra virgin olive oil, season with salt and pepper, scatter with thyme leaves, then sprinkle over the Parmesan. Arrange on a baking sheet and cook in the preheated oven for about 20 minutes or so until the aubergine/eggplant is soft and the skin is crisp.

Meanwhile, make the tomato sauce. Heat the oil in a large frying pan/skillet over low–medium heat and cook the onion and garlic for about 15 minutes until softened but not coloured. Add the cherry tomatoes and the wine. Stir in the sugar, season with salt and pepper and let the mixture bubble gently for about 20 minutes. Add the torn basil, and leave to bubble for another 10 minutes until the sauce is thick and sticky.

Spoon a little of the sauce onto each piece of aubergine/eggplant, top with a bocconcini and a small basil leaf, securing everything with a cocktail stick/toothpick. Season and serve immediately.

Artichokes with Prosciutto

Simple, but delicious. Artichokes in olive oil are much nicer than the cheaper ones that come in sunflower or vegetable oil. Similarly simple to the Aubergine & Tomato Toothpicks on page 67, these make a nice change to fried cicchetti to accompany your pre-dinner drinks.

120 g/4 oz. prosciutto
1 x 190-g/6½-oz. jar artichoke pieces in olive oil, drained

Serves 4

Put a little swirl of ham on top of each piece of artichoke and gently skewer with a cocktail stick/toothpick. Serve at once.

Dried Tomatoes, Fresh Anchovies & Sizzled Sage

Baby plum tomatoes are best here, rather than cherry tomatoes. Long, slow cooking is best, too, so you could cook overnight on a very low heat setting. Please take the quantities as a rough guide and adjust as needed.

1 kg/2 lbs. 4 oz. baby plum tomatoes, halved
3 tablespoons extra virgin olive oil
1 tablespoon white sugar
handful of fresh young sage leaves
150 g/5 oz. marinated (white) anchovies
sea salt and freshly ground black pepper
sunflower oil, for frying

Makes about 30

Preheat the oven to 170°C (325°F) Gas 3.

Arrange the tomatoes in a single layer on baking sheets. Drizzle with extra virgin olive oil and scatter over the sugar. Season with salt and pepper and bake ior a couple of hours (or overnight on the lowest heat setting) until sticky.

Heat the oil in the wok or deep fryer to 190°C (375°F), or until a piece of bread, dropped in the oil, sizzles and turns golden in a few seconds.

Fry the sage leaves for a few seconds until crisp and golden. Drain on paper towels.

Arrange little stacks of tomatoes and top with an anchovy and a sizzled sage leaf. Secure with a cocktail stick/toothpick and serve at once.

Chargrilled Vegetable Rotolini

Chargrilling vegetables gives them a wonderful deep, slightly smoky flavour, and when you roll them around other complementary ingredients, you have a sure-fire winner. Here are three simple recipes that make for great aperitivi or perfect appetizers.

Aubergine, Pesto, Tomatoes & Mozzarella

20 baby plum tomatoes, halved
4–5 tablespoons extra virgin olive oil
1 long aubergine/eggplant, thinly sliced lengthways
6 tablespoons Pesto (page 89)
250 g/9 oz. buffalo mozzarella, sliced
sea salt and freshly ground black pepper

Makes about 10

Preheat the oven to 150°C (300°F) Gas 2.

Drizzle the tomatoes with a little oil in a roasting pan and season with salt and pepper. Roast in the oven for about an hour until they are semi-dried.

Preheat a ridged grill pan until hot and cook the aubergine/eggplant slices on both sides until softened, turning to create a cross-hatch pattern. Season lightly and spread with pesto. Top with dried tomatoes and a slice of mozzarella and roll up.

Courgette, Blue Cheese & Rocket

3–4 courgettes/zucchini, thinly sliced lengthways
200 g/7 oz. Gorgonzola
2–3 handfuls of fresh rocket/ arugula
sea salt and freshly ground black pepper
fresh basil or mint leaves, to garnish

Makes about 16

Preheat a ridged grill pan until really hot and cook the courgette/zucchini slices on both sides, until softened, giving them a quarter turn to create a cross-hatch pattern.

When all the slices are cooked, spread with the Gorgonzola. Top with rocket/arugula, season with salt and pepper, then roll up.

Transfer to the serving platter, garnish with fresh basil or mint leaves and serve.

Romano Peppers, Black Olive Paste & Mozzarella

3 Romano peppers
4 tablespoons black olive paste
12 anchovy fillets (optional)
250 g/9 oz. buffalo mozzarella
sea salt and freshly ground black pepper

Makes 12

Carefully put the peppers directly over a medium flame on a gas stove and cook until the skin is blackened all over. Alternatively you could use an overhead grill/broiler. Once they are blackened all over, pop them into a plastic bag and leave to cool. The peppers should be soft and the blackened skin should come away very easily.

Cut into four lengths. Season lightly and spread each length with a little olive paste. Top with an anchovy (if using) and a slice of mozzarella and roll up to serve.

Artichokes with Taleggio Cheese & Prosciutto

This delicious recipes uses whole baby artichoke hearts that come in jars 'sottolio' (under oil), which makes them much quicker to rustle up than if you prepared fresh artichokes. However, if you have a glut of fresh artichokes, simply prepare them in the usual way and cook them in boiling salted water until soft. Taleggio is a semi-soft washed-rind cheese from Lombardy in northern Italy. Its mild flavour and creamy texture work so well with the salty prosciutto – a delectable mouthful.

8 whole baby artichokes in oil,
    drained
160 g/5½ oz. Taleggio cheese
8 slices prosciutto ham
3 tablespoons plain/all-purpose flour
sunflower oil, for deep-frying
lemon juice and sea salt flakes,
    to serve

FOR THE PASTELLA
1 egg white, beaten
130 ml/½ cup sparkling water
100 g/¾ cup self-raising/rising flour
grated zest of 1 lemon
sea salt

Makes 16

Remove the artichokes from the oil and dry them on paper towels. Gently make a hole in the centre of each one using a teaspoon or little finger. Push a small amount of Taleggio into the hole. Wrap each artichoke with a slice of prosciutto and set aside.

To make the pastella, whisk the egg white and sparkling water together. Slowly add the self-raising/rising flour and beat until smooth. Season with salt and stir in the grated lemon zest.

Dust the prepared artichokes in the plain/all-purpose flour and shake off any excess.

Heat the oil in the wok or deep fryer to 190°C (375°F), or until a piece of bread, dropped in the oil, sizzles and turns golden in a few seconds.

Dip the floured artichokes into the pastella and deep-fry for 3–4 minutes until golden and crisp. Drain on paper towels.

Squeeze over some fresh lemon juice, add a scattering of sea salt flakes, slice in half and serve immediately.

Wild Mushroom & Parma Ham Tartlets

These tasty, pastry-free tartlets are great for everyone who loves the classic ham and egg combo, while the porcini mushrooms add a lovely depth of flavour.

20 g/scant 1 cup dried porcini
  mushrooms
180 g/6 oz. thinly sliced Parma ham
6 eggs
50 g/⅔ cup grated Parmesan
4–5 young fresh sage leaves, chopped
small handful of chopped flat-leaf
  parsley
sea salt and freshly ground black
  pepper

6-cup muffin pan, lightly oiled

Makes 6

Soak the porcini mushrooms in boiling water for 20 minutes or so, then drain and coarsely chop.

Preheat the oven to 150°C (300°F) Gas 2.

Carefully line the prepared muffin pan with the slices of ham, taking care not to leave any gaps that the egg might trickle through!

In a large mixing bowl, beat the eggs until smooth. Add the chopped mushrooms, remaining ingredients and season with salt and pepper. Divide the egg mixture among the lined pan holes and bake in the preheated oven for about 25 minutes until the egg has set.

Remove from the oven, turn out and serve.

Arancini, Crocchette e Fritti

Rosemary & Asiago Arancini

Arancini are little golden balls of delight made from left-over risotto, usually with a little cheese or meat ragù hidden in the centre. You can use any left-over risotto you happen to have but I have also included a good recipe for one if needed. Mozzarella is the cheese most often used in the centre of arancini, but Asiago – a lovely cheese from the Veneto region of Italy that has DOP certification – is used here. The result is lighter and lovelier arancini that make ideal aperitivo nibbles.

800–850 ml/3¼–3½ cups good-quality vegetable stock
3 tablespoons extra virgin olive oil
1 onion, chopped
70 g/4½ tablespoons butter
400 g/2 cups risotto rice (arborio or carnaroli)
120 ml/½ cup white wine
100 g/1½ cups finely grated Parmesan
2 tablespoons finely chopped fresh rosemary
200 g/7 oz. Asiago (or other mild Italian cheese), cut into 1-cm/⅜-inch cubes
50 g/⅓ cups fine quick-cook polenta
sunflower oil, for deep-frying

FOR THE PASTELLA
1 egg white
30 ml/2 tablespoons sparkling water
30 g/⅓ cup self-raising/rising flour

Makes about 24

To make the risotto, heat the stock in a saucepan until very hot but not boiling. Heat the extra virgin olive oil in a frying pan/skillet over low–medium heat and sauté the onion gently for 10 minutes until soft but not coloured.

Add 20 g/1⅓ tablespoons of the butter to the pan and pour in the rice. Stir gently until all the rice grains are shiny and coated in butter. Add the wine, and stir until it has been absorbed. Add the stock, a ladleful at a time, stirring gently in between each addition, until the rice is cooked and the stock has all been absorbed. Stir in the remaining butter, the Parmesan and the chopped rosemary. Leave the risotto until completely cold. It helps to make the risotto several hours in advance, or even the day before – you can speed up the cooling process by spreading the risotto onto a baking sheet.

To make the pastella, whisk the egg white, stir in the sparkling water, then add the flour and stir until smooth.

Form the rice into balls the size of a large walnut, and push a cube of Asiago cheese into the centre of each one. Roll the arancini in the pastella, then coat lightly with the polenta.

Heat the oil in the wok or deep fryer to 190°C (375°F), or until a piece of bread, dropped in the oil, sizzles and turns golden in a few seconds. Fry the arancini for 3–4 minutes until crisp and golden. Drain on paper towels and serve immediately.

Pecorino, Porcini & Mozzarella Arancini

These delicious risotto balls can, of course, be made from leftover risotto, if you have any. They can also be prepared and rolled in advance; coat them in breadcrumbs and fry just before serving.

15 g/½ oz. dried porcini mushrooms

1 tablespoon olive oil

2 tablespoons unsalted butter

2 shallots, finely chopped

1 fat garlic clove, crushed

250 g/1¼ cups risotto rice (arborio or carnaroli)

800–850 ml/3¼–3½ cups good-quality vegetable stock

40 g/⅓ cup grated Pecorino

1 tablespoon freshly chopped flat-leaf parsley or oregano

125 g/4 oz. mozzarella, diced

100 g/¾ cup plain/all-purpose flour

2 eggs, lightly beaten

200 g/2 cups fresh fine breadcrumbs

sea salt and freshly ground black pepper

sunflower oil, for deep-frying

Makes 15–18

Soak the porcini in boiling water for about 15 minutes, or until soft. Drain well on paper towels and finely chop.

Heat the olive oil and butter in a medium saucepan and add the shallots, garlic and chopped porcini. Cook over low–medium heat until soft but not coloured. Add the rice to the pan and stir to coat well in the buttery mixture. Add the stock, a ladleful at a time, stirring gently in between each addition, until the rice is cooked and the stock has all been absorbed. Remove the pan from the heat, add the pecorino and herbs and season with salt and pepper. Leave until completely cold. It helps to make the risotto several hours in advance, or even the day before – you can speed up the cooling process by spreading the risotto onto a baking sheet.

Form the rice into balls the size of a large walnut. Taking one ball at a time, flatten it into a disc in the palm of your hand, press some diced mozzarella in the middle and wrap the rice around it to completely encase the cheese. Shape into a neat ball. Repeat with the remaining risotto.

Tip the flour, beaten eggs and breadcrumbs into separate shallow bowls. Roll the rice balls first in the flour, then coat well in the eggs and finally, roll them in the breadcrumbs to coat completely.

Heat the oil in the wok or deep fryer to 190°C (375°F), or until a piece of bread, dropped in the oil, sizzles and turns golden in a few seconds. Fry the arancini for 3–4 minutes until crisp and golden. Drain on paper towels and serve immediately.

Blue Cheese Arancini & Griddled Olives

Serve these blue cheese arancini and charred olives with a zingy Amaretto Sour (page 41) and you have the perfect pre-dinner small bite and drink selection.

FOR THE BLUE CHEESE ARANCINI
400 g/2 cups risotto rice (arborio or carnaroli)
100 g/1½ cups finely grated Parmesan
6 eggs, lightly beaten
100 g/3½ oz. blue cheese
75 g/generous ½ cup plain/all-purpose flour, seasoned
100 g/1¼ cups fine dried breadcrumbs
vegetable oil, for deep-frying
sea salt and black pepper

FOR THE GRIDDLED OLIVES
200 g/7 oz. large buttery green olives in brine, stoned/pitted and drained
2 tablespoons olive oil
1 teaspoon mixed dried herbs
pinch of dried chilli flakes/hot red pepper flakes
1 garlic clove, crushed
100 g/3½ oz. semi-dried/sunblush tomatoes

wooden skewers

Makes 24

Cook the rice in a large saucepan of boiling, salted water for 15 minutes, or until tender, then drain well, place in a large bowl and leave to cool. Add the Parmesan and two-thirds of the eggs, season generously and stir to combine. Spread the rice out on a tray until cool, then chill until cold.

Place 1 tablespoon of the cold rice mixture in the palm of your hand and flatten with a spoon. Place ½ teaspoon of the blue cheese in the centre of the rice and gently form the rice mixture around the filling to create a ball. Transfer the arancini to a plate. Repeat with the remaining rice mixture and blue cheese – you should make about 24 arancini.

Put the flour, remaining egg and breadcrumbs in separate bowls. Roll each arancini in the flour, dip in the egg, then roll in the breadcrumbs. Place on a tray and chill until needed.

Heat the oil in the wok or deep fryer to 190°C (375°F), or until a piece of bread, dropped in the oil, sizzles and turns golden in a few seconds. Fry the arancini for 3–4 minutes until crisp and golden. Drain on paper towels and serve immediately.

For the griddled olives, mix all the ingredients in a bowl, except for the semi-dried tomatoes. Thread the coated olives onto wooden skewers, place them on a flat surface and press them with something heavy to flatten them.

Heat a griddle pan until hot. Grill the olive skewers on the hot pan, pressing them again with something heavy, until the grill pattern is printed on the underside of the olives. Turn over and press again.

Remove from the skewers, transfer to a bowl with the garlic and semi-dried tomatoes and serve with the hot arancini.

Pecorino Arancini with Roasted Cherry Tomato Sauce

Classic, moreish, crowd-pleasing and just simply delicious. You can stuff these arancini with an array of fillings, from mozzarella to goat's cheese or chopped ham.

50 ml/3½ tablespoons olive oil
1 onion, finely chopped
2 garlic cloves, crushed
200 g/1 cup risotto rice (arborio or carnaroli)
750 ml/3 cups vegetable stock
5 lemon thyme sprigs, leaves picked
150 g/5 oz. pecorino (⅔ grated and ⅓ cut into 20 cubes)
100 g/scant ½ cup ricotta
½ teaspoon ground nutmeg
plain/all-purpose flour, for coating
2 eggs, lightly beaten
250 g/4½ cups fresh fine white breadcrumbs
sunflower oil, for deep-frying

FOR THE ROASTED CHERRY TOMATO SAUCE
500 g/1 lb. 2 oz. cherry tomatoes on the vine
4 garlic cloves, smashed
3 tablespoons olive oil
2 tablespoons honey
pinch of dried chilli flakes/hot red pepper flakes
sea salt and freshly ground black pepper
lemon thyme leaves, to garnish

Serves 4–6

Heat the oil in a saucepan over low heat, add onion and stir occasionally until tender. Add the crushed garlic and the rice, stir to coat, then add the stock, little by little, until rice is slightly overcooked and stock is absorbed. Add the thyme, grated pecorino, ricotta and nutmeg and stir until creamy. Remove from the heat and spread the mixture out in a tray. Cool to room temperature, then refrigerate for 1–1½ hours.

Meanwhile, make the sauce. Preheat the oven to 180°C (350°F) Gas 4. In a baking dish add the tomatoes on the vine with the garlic cloves, 2 tablespoons of the olive oil, honey, dried chilli flakes/hot red pepper flakes and salt and pepper. Roast in the preheated oven for 25 minutes, then add a few tablespoons of water, remove the vine and crush the tomatoes. Set aside.

Shape walnut-sized balls of the chilled rice mixture with your hands, then push a pecorino cube into centre of each, pressing rice around to enclose completely. Roll the rice balls in flour, then in beaten egg and finally in breadcrumbs, shaking off excess in between, ensuring they are completely coated. Place on a tray and chill in the fridge for 30 minutes.

Heat the oil in the wok or deep fryer to 190°C (375°F), or until a piece of bread, dropped in the oil, sizzles and turns golden in a few seconds. Fry the arancini for 3–4 minutes until crisp and golden. Drain on paper towels.

Place the roasted cherry tomato sauce on serving plates, drizzle over the remaining olive oil and serve with the hot arancini on top, scattered with thyme.

Courgette & Parmesan Crocchette

Crocchette, or croquettes, are delightfully crisp on the outside and fluffy in the middles. This recipe combines the fresh flavour of courgettes/zucchini with rich Parmesan cheese in a potato croquette that is just waiting to be dipped into a sweet and spicy sauce.

200 g/7 oz. courgettes/zucchini, coarsely grated
1 teaspoon salt
500 g/1 lb. 2 oz. potatoes, scrubbed clean but not peeled
100 g/1½ cups finely grated Parmesan
1 egg, beaten
120 g/3 cups panko breadcrumbs
freshly ground black pepper
sunflower oil, for deep-frying

FOR THE CHILLI/CHILE JAM
1 kg/2 lbs. 4 oz. ripe tomatoes
8 fresh red chillies/chiles
3-cm/1¼-inch piece of fresh ginger, grated
100 ml/⅓ cup plus 1 tablespoon white wine vinegar
250 g/1¼ cups caster/granulated sugar
2 tablespoons extra virgin olive oil

sterilized glass jars

Makes about 12

First put the grated courgettes/zucchini into a colander or large sieve/strainer and sprinkle over the salt. Leave for 30 minutes or so until they start to ooze water. Squeeze as much liquid as possible out of them (or else you'll have sloppy croquettes!) and set aside.

Boil the potatoes in a large saucepan of salted water until they are soft all the way through when tested with a metal skewer or the thin blade of a knife. Drain and leave until cold enough to handle comfortably.

To make the chilli/chile jam, whizz the tomatoes and chillies/chiles to a purée in a food processor or blender. Transfer the mixture to a large saucepan and add the ginger, vinegar and sugar. Cook over low heat until the sugar has dissolved and then bubble for 30 minutes or so until the mixture has reduced and thickened. Add the extra virgin olive oil and cook for another 15 minutes or so until the mixture has the consistency of jam.

Peel the potatoes and coarsely grate them into a large bowl. Add the grated courgettes/zucchini and Parmesan, and stir in the beaten egg. Add a good grind of black pepper to season and form the mixture into small log shapes. Roll lightly in the panko breadcrumbs and set aside.

Heat the oil in the wok or deep fryer to 190°C (375°F), or until a piece of bread, dropped in the oil, sizzles and turns golden in a few seconds. Fry the crochette for 3–4 minutes until crisp and golden. Drain on paper towels and serve with the chilli/chile jam.

Store the left-over chilli/chile jam in sterilized glass jars in the fridge.

Speck & Smoked Ricotta Crocchette

It is possible to find unpleasant *crocchette* in Venice. Unfortunately, some of the not-so-hot *bacari* do resort to buying in their *cicchetti* rather than making them in house. On top of that they serve them cold from the counter, so the result is disappointing, to say the least. However, these lovely light, crisp *crocchette* are poles apart from those dodgy freezer-to-fryer specimens. Smoky Scamorza cheese, salty speck, fresh rosemary and a crunchy Parmesan and polenta coating make these little treats irresistible. They're lovely with the Roasted Cherry Tomato Sauce on page 80.

500 g/1 lb. 2 oz. floury potatoes
2 dried bay leaves
150 g/1⅓ cup grated Scamorza (smoked mozzarella)
100 g/¾ cup chopped speck ham
1 teaspoon finely chopped fresh rosemary
1 egg
sea salt and freshly ground black pepper
sunflower oil, for deep-frying
lemon wedges, to serve (optional)

FOR THE COATING
50 g/¾ cup finely grated Parmesan
75 g/½ cup fine quick-cook polenta

Makes about 10

Boil the potatoes in a large saucepan of salted water with the bay leaves, until they are soft all the way through when tested with a metal skewer or the thin blade of a knife. Drain and leave until cold enough to handle comfortably. The exact cooking time will vary according to the size of potatoes used. Once they are cold, peel away the skin and coarsely grate into a large mixing bowl.

Add the grated Scamorza, speck and rosemary, and gently stir everything until it is evenly mixed. Add the egg, mix again and season the mixture with salt and pepper. Form the mixture into mini log shapes and (if you have time) pop them in the fridge for 30 minutes to firm up.

For the coating, mix the Parmesan and polenta together, then roll the logs in the mixture to coat them evenly.

Heat the oil in the wok or deep fryer to 190°C (375°F), or until a piece of bread, dropped in the oil, sizzles and turns golden in a few seconds. Fry the crochette for 3–4 minutes until crisp and golden. Drain on paper towels.

Drain on paper towels and serve with lemon wedges.

Olive Supplì with Saffron Salt

Traditional *supplì* have mozzarella inside and are known in Rome as *supplì al telefono*, because when you bite into them the mozzarella pulls and looks like a telephone wire. A cured black olive is hidden in the centre of these, which makes for a delicious surprise.

16 cured black olives, pitted/stoned
40 g/¼ cup plain/all-purpose flour
2 eggs, beaten
140 g/1½ cups fresh fine
  breadcrumbs
vegetable oil, for deep-frying
saffron salt, to serve

FOR THE RISOTTO
20 g/½ cup dried porcini mushrooms
250 ml/1 cup white wine
500 ml/2 cups chicken stock
2 tablespoons olive oil
1 garlic clove, finely chopped
2 tablespoons fresh thyme leaves
1 tablespoon chopped fresh rosemary
200 g/1 cup risotto rice (arborio
  or carnaroli)
60 g/¾ cup grated Parmesan
cracked black pepper and sea salt

Makes 16

For the risotto, soak the mushrooms in the wine for 30 minutes. Drain, reserving the liquid, and chop roughly. Pour the reserved liquid into a small pan with the chicken stock. Bring to a boil, then reduce to a simmer.

Put the olive oil, garlic, thyme, rosemary, and mushrooms in a medium pan and cook over medium to high heat for a few seconds, coating with the olive oil. Add the rice and stir for 2–3 minutes until well coated and translucent. Start adding the stock a ladleful at a time, stirring continuously until the liquid has been absorbed. Continue until you have used all the liquid, about 20 minutes. Stir in the cheese and season with cracked black pepper and sea salt. Pour onto a large plate and spread out to cool.

To make the supplì, take tablespoons of cooled risotto and form 16 balls. With your forefinger make a dent in each risotto ball and place an olive in the center. Roll the risotto ball in your hand to reshape and cover the olive.

Dust the supplì balls with flour, dip into the beaten egg, and then toss in the breadcrumbs until well coated. At this stage they can be left to rest in the fridge for up to 6 hours until you are ready to cook.

Heat the oil in the wok or deep fryer to 180°C (350°F), or until a piece of bread, dropped in the oil, sizzles and turns golden in about 20 seconds.

Fry the supplì in batches until crispy and golden brown, about 2 minutes. Drain on paper towels. Sprinkle generously with saffron salt and serve.

Deep-fried Mozzarella Sticks

Warm, crispy, gooey cheese sticks are a great antidote to those particular munchies you get when it's not quite dinner time! Serve these with pre-dinner drinks and your friends and family will thank you for it!

2 eggs, beaten
120 g/1½ cups Italian-seasoned breadcrumbs
½ teaspoon garlic salt
80 g/⅔ cup plain/all-purpose flour
40 g/⅓ cup cornflour/cornstarch
450-g/1-lb. bag of mozzarella cheese sticks
vegetable oil, for deep-frying

Serves 4–6

In a small bowl, mix the beaten eggs with 60 ml/¼ cup water.

In a separate medium bowl, mix the breadcrumbs and garlic salt together. In another medium bowl, mix the flour and cornflour/cornstarch together.

Heat the oil in the wok or deep fryer to 180°C (350°F), or until a piece of bread, dropped in the oil, sizzles and turns golden in about 20 seconds.

One at a time, coat each mozzarella stick in flour, then egg and then breadcrumbs. Fry for about 30 seconds until golden brown. Drain on paper towels before serving.

Polenta Fries with Pesto

Even people who swear they don't like polenta will change their minds when they taste these crispy, golden 'fries', given some oomph with well-flavoured stock and lots of Parmesan.

500 ml/2 cups good-quality stock
125 g/¾ cup fine quick-cook polenta
30 g/2 tablespoons butter
50 g/⅔ cup finely grated Parmesan
sunflower oil, for frying

FOR THE PESTO
2 large handfuls of fresh basil leaves
2 garlic cloves
120 ml/½ cup extra virgin olive oil
grated zest of 1 lemon and juice of ½
50 g/⅔ cup finely grated Parmesan
sea salt flakes

baking sheet, oiled

Serves 6

Bring the stock to the boil in a saucepan, turn the heat down and slowly add the polenta, stirring all the time. Stir until the polenta is thick and smooth and comes away from the sides of the pan. Remove from the heat and stir in the butter and grated Parmesan.

Spread the polenta onto the prepared baking sheet to a depth of about 1 cm/⅜ inch. Leave to set and, when completely cold, cut into 'fries' using a sharp knife.

To make the pesto, put the basil, garlic and oil into a food processor and whizz. Add the lemon zest, juice and Parmesan. Whizz again and season.

Heat the oil in the wok or deep fryer to 190°C (375°F), or until a piece of bread, dropped in the oil, sizzles and turns golden in a few seconds.

Fry the fries for 3–4 minutes until golden and crisp. Drain on paper towels and serve immediately with the fresh basil pesto for dipping.

Pancetta & Fennel Puffs

These *coccoli* ('little darlings!') are a type of savoury doughnut or *bomboloni* flavoured with pancetta. This version contains lightly crushed fennel seeds, a flavouring that is very popular in Tuscany, especially with cured pork. They are deep-fried until crisp on the outside and soft inside and can be kept warm in the oven. Make sure they are piping hot and sprinkled liberally with sea salt when you serve them. These are especially wonderful if you have the chance to fry them in pure olive oil. The dough can also be rolled out thinly and cut into squares, then fried.

200 ml/¾ cup milk
50 g/2 oz. pure lard, roughly chopped
37 g/1½ cakes compressed fresh yeast or 1 packet fast-action dried yeast
400 g/3½ cups Italian '0' or '00' flour, or unbleached plain/all-purpose flour, plus extra if needed
50 g/2 oz. pancetta, finely diced
1 teaspoon fennel seeds, lightly crushed
sea salt
vegetable or olive oil, for deep-frying

Makes 30–40

Put the milk and lard in a saucepan and heat gently until the lard has melted. Don't let the milk get too hot. Crumble in the compressed yeast (if using) and beat until dissolved. Sift the flour and a good pinch of salt into a bowl and make a well in the centre. If you are using fast-action yeast, stir it into the flour now. Pour in the warm milk mixture and add the pancetta and fennel seeds. Mix to a soft dough, adding more flour, if necessary. Form into a ball, cover with clingfilm/plastic wrap or a damp kitchen towel and let rise for 2 hours, or until doubled in size.

Heat the oil in the wok or deep fryer to 180°C (350°F), or until a piece of bread, dropped in the oil, sizzles and turns golden in about 20 seconds.

Uncover the dough, punch out the air and knead for 1 minute. Pull off small walnut-sized pieces of dough, about 2 cm/¾ inch, and roll into rough balls.

Fry in batches for 2–3 minutes until pale brown and puffy. Drain well and tip onto paper towels. Sprinkle with salt and serve while still hot.

Thyme & Parmesan Choux Puffs

This is a winning flavour combination. The thyme and Parmesan choux buns can be made in advance and frozen before baking. Nothing smells nicer than pastry baking in the oven, so keep these in your freezer for impromptu aperitivo! The Negroni Sbagliato (page 18) is a classic Campari-based cocktail and the perfect accompanying drink for these tasty morsels.

5 large (US extra-large) eggs
80 g/¾ stick butter, cubed
1 teaspoon sea salt
150 g/generous 1 cup plain/
   all-purpose flour
¼ teaspoon freshly grated nutmeg
1 teaspoon mustard powder
pinch of cayenne pepper
4 thyme sprigs, leaves picked,
   plus extra to garnish
1 teaspoon honey
175 g/generous 2 cups grated
   Parmesan or pecorino
milk or water, for mixing

2 baking sheets, lined

Makes about 30

Preheat the oven to 220°C (425°F) Gas 7.

Crack 4 of the eggs into a jug/pitcher and beat together.

Put 250 ml/1 cup water, the butter and salt in a saucepan over medium heat and bring to a simmer, stirring occasionally, to help melt the butter.

Take the pan off the heat and pour in the flour, stirring until it comes together into a paste. Put the pan back over low heat, and stir until you have a smooth ball and the dough is starting to form a layer on the base of the pan; 2–3 minutes.

Take the pan off the heat and use a stand mixer or hand beaters to beat the dough for about 5 minutes until cooled.

Beat in the 4 beaten eggs, little by little, making sure each addition is well incorporated before adding the next. Stir in the nutmeg, mustard, cayenne, thyme, honey and two-thirds of the cheese.

Pipe or spoon the mixture onto the prepared baking sheets (you should get approximately 30 buns from the mixture).

Whisk together the last egg with a dash of water or milk, then brush onto the buns, sprinkle with the remaining cheese and place in the preheated oven. Reduce the oven temperature to 200°C (400°F) Gas 6 and bake for 20 minutes until puffed up and golden.

Remove from the oven, pierce the side of each one with a small knife and put back in the oven for 5 minutes to let the steam out, before removing and garnishing with thyme.

Puff Pastry Ricotta & Spinach Rolls

Tiny and tasty, these savoury rolls are made with the very typical Italian combination of spinach and ricotta. They are an Italian favourite, often served in bars, as a snack with an aperitivo.

450 g/1 lb. fresh spinach, trimmed
    and washed
150 g/5 oz. firm ricotta
50 g/¾ cup finely grated Parmesan
    or Grana Padano
300 g/10 oz. ready-rolled puff pastry,
    defrosted if frozen
plain/all-purpose flour, for dusting
1 egg beaten with 1 tablespoon milk
sea salt and freshly ground black
    pepper

Makes about 24

Preheat the oven to 200°C (400°F) Gas 6.

Put the spinach in a saucepan with just the water that clings to the leaves after washing. Cook over gentle heat for 2–3 minutes until wilted and collapsed. Spoon the spinach into a colander, squeeze out any moisture, then turn it out onto a board and chop it. Put it in a bowl and stir in the ricotta and Parmesan, then season with salt and pepper.

Lay out the pastry on a lightly floured work surface and cut into 3 rectangular pieces measuring 30 x 8 cm/12 x 3 inches. Spoon a line of the filling all the way along the length of one piece of pastry, about the same thickness as a sausage and slightly off-centre. Brush a little of the egg mixture along the narrower pastry border, then lift the other pastry edge over the filling to enclose it and seal the two edges together. Gently roll the whole thing over so that the seam sits underneath. Brush the top with the egg mixture. Repeat with the remaining pastry rectangles.

Cut each pastry roll into pieces about 2.5 cm/1 inch in length and place on a baking sheet. Bake for 6–8 minutes until puffed and golden. The rolls are best served freshly made and warm, but can be reheated if necessary.

Crostini, Panini e Tramazzini

Pea & Mint Crostini

Peas and mint make a heavenly combination, especially on crunchy *crostini*. These are best when peas are in season, but good-quality frozen ones are pretty good, too.

10–12 slices baguette
60 ml/¼ cup extra
   virgin olive oil
1 garlic clove
250 g/1⅔ cups fresh
   peas (or 250 g/2 cups
   frozen peas)
small handful of young
   fresh mint leaves,
roughly chopped,
   plus extra to garnish
sea salt
grated zest of 1 lemon,
   to garnish

Makes 10–12

Preheat the oven to 180°C (350°F) Gas 4.

Brush the baguette slices with a little of the oil and place on a baking sheet. Cook in the preheated oven for about 10 minutes until golden and crisp. Remove from the oven and rub lightly with the garlic clove.

If you're using fresh peas, cook them in boiling salted water for about 3 minutes, then drain and pop into a blender. If you're using frozen peas, simply defrost them and pop them straight into the blender. Add the remaining oil and whizz to a lightly textured purée. Remove from the blender and stir in the mint.

Form the pea mixture into neat quenelles using two teaspoons and top the crostini. Scatter with a little grated lemon zest and a few extra mint leaves, and serve.

Salt Cod Crostini

Most *bacari* serve some sort of *crostini* topped with salt cod. Soak the fish for 48 hours before blending, changing the water often. Laced with garlic and speckled with herbs, Baccalà con Aglio is a delight.

500 g/1 lb. 2 oz. salt
   cod, soaked for
   48 hours
570 ml/2¼ cups whole
   milk
2 fresh bay leaves
1 tablespoon black
   peppercorns
2 garlic cloves
120 ml/½ cup extra
   virgin olive oil, plus
   extra for brushing
handful of finely
   chopped flat-leaf
   parsley
12 slices baguette,
   baked as left
sea salt and freshly
   ground black pepper

Makes 12

Preheat the oven to 180°C (350°F) Gas 4.

Place the pre-soaked cod in a large saucepan with the milk. Add the bay leaves, peppercorns, garlic and enough water to cover the fish. Set over medium heat and simmer for 20 minutes until just cooked. Remove the fish and let cool. Strain the milk, reserving the milk and the garlic.

When the fish has cooled a little, flake it carefully into the bowl of a food processor or blender, taking care to remove the bones. Add half of the olive oil, a little of the reserved milk and the softened garlic. Pulse, adding the remaining oil and as much milk as necessary, until the mixture has a similar thickness to creamy mashed potato.

Stir in the parsley, adjust the seasoning and use it to top the crostini.

Gorgonzola & Anchovy Crostini
with Pickled Radicchio

This seemingly unassuming crostini is topped only with Gorgonzola cheese, a single anchovy and some pickled radicchio – it is utterly sublime. It's a quick pickle that can be prepared in minutes and simply needs cooling rather than storing in sterilized glass jars. The lovely sweet and sour flavour with a hint of fennel seed makes it even better. More often than not, Venetian *crostini* bases are simply slices of baguette. You can toast the slices on a griddle, or bake them in the oven with a little slick of olive oil to give them a lovely crunch that highlights the flavour of the topping even more.

12 slices small baguette
3–4 tablespoons extra virgin olive oil
300 g/2½ cups Gorgonzola
12 canned anchovies

FOR THE PICKLED RADICCHIO
300 ml/1¼ cups apple vinegar
1 generous tablespoon runny honey
1 teaspoon fennel seeds
1 small long radicchio/Italian chicory, sliced

Makes 12

To pickle the radicchio, pour the apple vinegar into a large saucepan and bring to the boil. Boil for a couple of minutes, then add the honey and fennel seeds. Turn the heat down and bubble for 5 minutes. Drop the sliced radicchio into the vinegar, cook for 1 minute, then turn off the heat. After 4–5 minutes, remove the radicchio and fennel seeds with a slotted spoon, transfer to a mixing bowl and let cool.

Brush the baguette slices with the oil and toast on a hot griddle pan until golden (alternatively bake in a hot oven for 5 minutes or so).

Top each slice with a good dollop of Gorgonzola cheese and add a single anchovy. Top with some of the pickled radicchio and serve.

Polenta Crostini with Caramelized Fennel & Prawns

Mixed with good-quality vegetable stock, butter and some Parmesan, and then griddled until crisp, polenta makes a brilliant base for crostini. Don't skip the sprinkling of sugar when roasting the fennel, and be sure cook the crostini until caramel coloured.

juice of 2 lemons
2 bulbs of Florence fennel, trimmed and cut into wedges
2 teaspoons white sugar
50 ml/3½ tablespoons extra virgin olive oil, plus extra for frying
2 garlic cloves, finely chopped
grated zest and juice of ½ lemon
20 raw jumbo prawns/shrimp, peeled and deveined
sea salt and freshly ground black pepper
1 tablespoon chopped fresh chives (or a few fennel fronds), to garnish

FOR THE POLENTA CROSTINI
500 ml/2 cups good-quality vegetable stock
125 g/¾ cup fine quick-cook polenta
30 g/2 tablespoons butter
50 g/¾ cup finely grated Parmesan

baking sheet, oiled

Makes 20

For the polenta crostini, heat the stock in a saucepan until boiling. Turn the heat down slightly and slowly add the polenta, stirring all the time. Continue to stir until the polenta is thick and smooth, and comes away from the sides of the pan. Remove from the heat and stir in the butter and Parmesan. Spoon onto the prepared baking sheet and spread out to about 1 cm/⅜ inch deep. Leave to set.

When the polenta is completely cold, cut into circles 3 cm/1¼ inches in diameter using the top of a small glass.

Preheat the oven to 190°C (375°F) Gas 5.

Fill a saucepan with water and add the juice of ½ lemon. Drop the wedges of fennel into the acidulated water. Bring to the boil, turn the heat down and simmer for 10 minutes. Drain the fennel and lay it in a single layer on a baking sheet. Squeeze over the remaining lemon juice, scatter over the sugar and season. Roast for 25–30 minutes until golden.

Meanwhile, bring a large pan of salted water to the boil. Mix the extra virgin olive oil, garlic, lemon zest and juice together in a large bowl and season to taste. Drop the prawns/shrimp into the boiling water and cook for 2 minutes, until pink and lightly cooked. Lift them from the pan with a slotted spoon and drop them straight into the oil mixture. Stir and cool.

To assemble the crostini, brush the polenta bases with a little oil and cook on a hot griddle pan until golden. Top each with the caramelized fennel and a prawn/shrimp. Garnish with chopped chives or fennel fronds and serve.

White Bean & Black Olive Crostini

The combination of bland creamy beans and sharp, rich, salty tapenade makes a sublime mouthful, especially on crisp *crostini* and when accompanied by a refreshing aperitvo.

FOR THE TAPENADE
175 g/6 oz. Greek-style black olives, such as Kalamata, pitted
2 garlic cloves
3 canned anchovies, drained
2 teaspoons capers, drained
1 tablespoon olive oil

FOR THE CROSTINI
1 Italian sfilatino or thin French baguette, sliced into thin rounds
extra virgin olive oil, for brushing

FOR THE WHITE BEAN PURÉE
2 tablespoons olive oil
2 garlic cloves, finely chopped
1 teaspoon very finely chopped fresh rosemary
1 small red chilli/chile, deseeded and finely chopped
400-g/14-oz. can cannellini beans, drained and rinsed
sea salt and freshly ground black pepper

TO SERVE
freshly chopped parsley

Serves 6–8

To make the tapenade, put the olives, garlic, anchovies, capers and olive oil into a blender or food processor and blend until smooth. Scrape out into a jar, cover with a layer of olive oil and set aside.

Preheat the oven to 190°C (375°F) Gas 5.

To make the crostini, brush both sides of each slice of bread with olive oil and spread out on a baking sheet. Bake for about 10 minutes until crisp and golden.

Meanwhile, make the bean purée. Heat the oil in a small frying pan/skillet and add the garlic. Cook gently for 2 minutes until golden but don't let it turn brown. Stir in the rosemary and chilli/chile. Remove from the heat, add the beans and 3 tablespoons of water. Mash the beans roughly with a fork and return to the heat until warmed through. Taste and season with salt and pepper.

Spread a layer of tapenade on the crostini followed by a spoonful of bean purée. Sprinkle with chopped parsley and serve immediately.

Tuna, Black Olive, Pine Nut & Caper Crostini

The contrast of strong flavours and interesting textures in this recipe transports you instantly to the shores of the Mediterranean. Use a mixture of green and black olives if you prefer a sharper flavour. This mixture can be used as a stuffing for tomatoes, too.

175 g/6 oz. oven-baked or
  Greek-style black olives, pitted
  and chopped
2 tablespoons pine nuts, chopped
1 tablespoon capers, rinsed and
  chopped
1 small garlic clove, finely chopped
1 tablespoon freshly chopped parsley
6 sun-dried tomatoes, soaked and
  chopped
1 tablespoon finely grated lemon zest
100 g/3½ oz. (drained weight) canned
  tuna in oil, drained
sea salt and freshly ground black
  pepper
extra virgin olive oil, for moistening

FOR THE CROSTINI
1 Italian sfilatino or thin French
  baguette, thinly sliced diagonally
extra virgin olive oil, for brushing

Serves 6

Preheat the oven to 190°C (375°F) Gas 5.

To make the crostini, brush both sides of each slice of bread with olive oil and spread out on a baking sheet. Bake for about 10 minutes until crisp and golden.

Put the olives, pine nuts, capers, garlic, parsley, tomatoes and lemon zest in a bowl and mix well. Add the tuna, break it up with a fork and mix it thoroughly with the other ingredients. Moisten with a little olive oil, taste and season with salt and pepper.

Pile the mixture on top of the crostini. Serve immediately.

Tramazzini Misti

It's said that these little cocktail size crustless sandwiches were invented at Harry's Bar in Venice, although they are found all over Italy. These suggested fillings all serve four.

Parma Ham, Pear & Rocket

small loaf of white bread, thickly sliced
3–4 tablespoons extra virgin olive oil
12 slices Parma ham
1 small ripe pear, peeled and sliced
2 small handfuls of rocket/ arugula
30 g/1 oz. Parmesan shavings
1 tablespoon balsamic vinegar

Drizzle the bread with a little olive oil. Lay the Parma ham over half the bread slices.

Toss the pear, rocket/arugula and cheese gently together with the remaining olive oil and the balsamic vinegar.

Top the ham with a little of the pear mixture and sandwich together with the remaining bread slices. Trim off the crusts, cut into triangles or fingers and serve at once.

Note You could try San Daniele or Speck instead of Parma ham, or Grana Padano or an aged pecorino rather than Parmesan.

Egg & Asparagus

4 eggs
small bunch of asparagus
4–5 tablespoons mayonnaise
grated zest of 1 lemon
small bunch of chives, chopped
small loaf of white bread, thickly sliced
sea salt and freshly ground black pepper

Cook the eggs in boiling water until almost hard boiled. Leave until cold, peel and chop the eggs roughly.

Cook the asparagus in a large pan of boiling water for about 2–3 minutes until just soft. Remove from the water, cool and chop into small pieces.

Mix the mayonnaise and lemon zest together. Fold in the asparagus, eggs and chives and season with salt and pepper.

Spread the filling over half the bread slices and top with another slice. Trim off the crusts, cut into triangles or fingers and serve at once.

Crab Mayonnaise & Watercress

4–5 tablespoons mayonnaise
grated zest of 1 lemon
2 fairly large dressed crabs
small loaf of white bread, thickly sliced
2 handfuls of watercress, trimmed

Mix the mayonnaise and lemon zest together. Turn the white crabmeat into a bowl and stir in enough of the lemon mayonnaise to bind it.

Spread all the bread slices with the brown crabmeat. Spread the white crab mixture over half of the slices and add a layer of watercress.

Place another slice of bread on each. Trim off the crusts, cut into triangles or fingers and serve at once.

Mini Sandwiches

Turning toasted sandwiches and panini into perfectly formed mini mouthfuls is ideal for serving with drinks. Try your favourite fillers or opt for one of these ideas. Each recipe makes 12.

Little Cheese & Ham Toasties Florian Style

6 large slices of white bread
200 g/1 cup Robiolino (or other buttery cream cheese)
6 thin slices cooked ham
150 g/5 oz. Asiago (or other mild Italian cheese), grated
50 g/3½ tablespoons butter, softened

Preheat the oven to 190°C (375°F) Gas 5.

Spread the bread with Robiolino on one side. Lay ham over three of the slices and top with the grated Asiago cheese. Sandwich together with the remaining slices of bread and spead the outer sides with butter. Put on a baking sheet and bake in the preheated oven for 10–15 minutes, until golden.

Remove from the oven and cut off the crusts. Eat quite a few of the crusts whilst cutting the sandwiches into small squares. Thread two sandwiches onto each skewer and serve immediately.

Roasted Veg & Mozzarella Clubs

2 small courgettes/zucchini
1 small aubergine/eggplant
3 tablespoons olive oil
jar of sun-dried tomatoes
125 g/4½ oz. mozzarella, sliced
small bunch of fresh basil
9 thick slices white bread
200 g/1 cup cream cheese
50 g/3½ tablespoons butter, softened
sea salt and freshly ground black pepper

Preheat the oven to 190°C (375°F) Gas 5.

Slice the courgettes/zucchini and aubergine/eggplant. Toss with the oil in mixing bowl. Heat a griddle pan and griddle the slices until just cooked. Season and leave to cool.

Spread half of the bread with soft cheese. Add the vegetables, sun-dried tomatoes, mozzarella and basil, placing an extra slice of bread in the centre. Spread the outside slices of bread with butter; put on a baking sheet.

Bake for 10–15 minutes until golden. Cut into small triangles.

Mini Panini

12 mini ciabatta rolls

FILLING SUGGESTIONS
salsciccia picante e robiola (pepperoni sausage and cream cheese)
Gorgonzola dolce e noci (Gorgonzola and walnut)
coppa di Parma (cured pork loin)
manzo fume, crema di asparagi e rucola (smoked beef, creamed asparagus and rocket/arugula)
verdure Mediterranea grigliate (grilled Mediterranean vegetables)

Slice open the ciabatta rolls, top the bases with your chosen filling and lay the lids on top.

Thread onto a small skewer to hold everything together and serve.

Grilled Fig & Prosciutto Bruschetta with Rocket

This combination of caramelized figs and crisply barbecued prosciutto on crisp bruschetta is simply irresistible. The figs are best cooked on a barbecue, but you can use a stovetop grill pan or a grill – just get the right amount of charring on the figs.

4 thick slices country bread, preferably sourdough
2 garlic cloves, halved
8 ripe fresh figs
2 tablespoons balsamic vinegar
12 slices prosciutto
100 g/1 cup rocket/arugula
sea salt and freshly ground black pepper
extra virgin olive oil, for drizzling and brushing
Parmesan shavings, to serve

Serves 4

To make the bruschetta, grill, toast or pan-grill the bread on both sides until lightly charred or toasted. Rub the top side of each slice with the cut garlic, then drizzle with olive oil. Keep them warm in a low oven.

Take the figs and stand them upright. Using a small, sharp knife, make two cuts across each fig not quite quartering it, but keeping it intact at the base. Ease the figs open and brush with balsamic vinegar and olive oil.

Put the figs cut-side down on a preheated barbecue or stovetop grill pan and cook for 3–4 minutes until hot and slightly charred – don't move them during cooking. Alternatively, place the figs cut-side up under a really hot grill/broiler until browning and heated through.

While the figs are cooking, place half the slices of prosciutto on the barbecue or stove-top grill pan, or under the grill/broiler and cook until frazzled. Remove and keep warm while cooking the remaining slices.

Place two figs, three pieces of prosciutto and some rocket/arugula on each slice of bruschetta. Cover with Parmesan shavings and drizzle with olive oil. Serve immediately.

'Nduja & Black Olive Tapenade Mini Pizzette

The name 'tapenade' comes from the Provençal word *tapena* meaning 'capers' and is a thick sauce or spread made from capers, garlic and anchovies. This recipe adds rich dark olives and charred sweet (bell) pepper for a more intense, smoky flavour that is delicious with fiery 'nduja. Spread the rest on focaccia or add more oil for a dipping sauce.

½ recipe Basic Pizza Dough (page 110), making just 1 ball of dough
250–300 g/9–10 oz. 'nduja (spicy Calabrian sausage)
12 cherry tomatoes, halved
sea salt and freshly ground black pepper
extra virgin olive oil, for brushing
fresh oregano, to garnish

FOR THE TAPENADE
1 small sweet red (bell) pepper
3 garlic cloves, skins on
2–3 tablespoons salted capers
225 g/8 oz. black wrinkly olives, stoned/pitted
12 boneless anchovy fillets
about 150 ml/⅔ cup mild olive oil
fresh lemon juice, to taste
3 tablespoons chopped fresh parsley
freshly ground black pepper

round cookie cutter, 7 cm/3 inches (optional)
baking sheet, lightly oiled

Makes 12

Preheat the oven to 220°C (425°F) Gas 7.

First make the tapenade. Put the whole (bell) pepper and garlic cloves under a hot grill/broiler and grill/broil for about 15 minutes, turning until completely charred all over. Cool, rub off the skin (do not wash) and remove the stalk and seeds from the pepper. Peel the skin off the garlic. Rinse the capers and drain. Put all these in a food processor with the olives and anchovies and process until roughly chopped. With the motor running, slowly add the olive oil until you have a fairly smooth dark paste (process less if you prefer it rougher). Season with lemon juice and black pepper. Stir in the parsley. Use immediately or store in a jar, covered with a layer of olive oil to exclude the air, for up to 1 month.

Uncover the dough, punch out the air and roll or pull very thinly on a well-floured surface. Using an upturned glass or a cookie cutter, stamp out twelve 7-cm/3-inch circles and lay on a lightly oiled baking sheet.

Spread the pizzette with a little black olive tapenade and top with a heaped teaspoon of 'nduja. Push in halved cherry tomatoes then brush with olive oil. Season if necessary and bake for 8–10 minutes. Serve immediately garnished with fresh oregano.

Pancetta & Pecorino Pizzette

These mini pizzas are quite filling, so they're ideal for serving with drinks when you need something a little more than a nibble but less than a full-size pizza! The perfect mouthful for aperitivo.

FOR THE DOUGH

170 g/1½ cups plain/all-purpose or wholemeal/whole-wheat flour, plus extra for dusting
small pinch of fast-action/rapid-rise yeast
1 tablespoon olive oil
pinch of sea salt
1 teaspoon caster/granulated sugar

FOR THE TOPPING

1 tablespoon olive oil
300 g/10 oz. pancetta, thinly sliced or diced
400-g/14-oz. can of tomatoes, drained and chopped
big pinch of freshly chopped parsley
big pinch of freshly chopped or dried oregano
1 tablespoon tomato purée/paste
200 g/7 oz. pecorino or Parmesan, grated or shaved
sea salt and freshly ground black pepper

large baking sheet, greased or lined

Makes 6

Preheat the oven to 180°C (350°F) Gas 4.

For the dough, put all the ingredients in a bowl, add 125 ml/½ cup water and mix together with your hands to make a dough. If the mixture feels sloppy, just add a little more flour, or add a little more water for the opposite (it shouldn't be so dry that it crumbles when you roll it). Turn the dough out onto a flour-dusted surface and knead for 5–10 minutes until smooth and elastic.

Divide the dough into six even pieces. On a flour-dusted surface, roll out each portion of dough into an oval. Place on the prepared baking sheet and bake in the preheated oven for 10 minutes, turning over halfway through.

Meanwhile, prepare the topping. Heat the olive oil in a frying pan/skillet. Add the pancetta and fry over medium heat until fully cooked – let it brown but don't reduce it right down at this stage because it will continue to bake on top of the pizzettes. Put the canned tomatoes, parsley, oregano and tomato purée/paste into a bowl, season with salt and pepper and mix well.

Once the pizza bases/crusts are initially baked, remove from the oven. Spread the tomato mixture over the top of the bases/crusts. Put the pancetta pieces on top, then sprinkle over the cheese.

Return the pizzettes to the preheated oven on the middle shelf (ideally, put the pizzettes directly onto the oven shelf, rather than using the baking sheet, so the bases can continue to crisp) and bake for a further 15 minutes until the cheese has melted. Serve hot.

Fresh Fig, Whipped Goat's Cheese, Ricotta & Rocket Pizza

A thin and crispy pizza base, topped with creamy goat's cheese, juicy syrupy figs and blackberries. The blackberries add a juicy, sweet tartness but any soft berry can be used here, whatever is in season. It is equally delicious if you only have figs. Cut it into small slices and serve with drinks.

FOR THE DOUGH

5 g/1 teaspoon dried yeast

50 ml/3½ tablespoons lukewarm water

350 g/2½ cups strong white bread flour, plus extra for dusting

1 tablespoon sea salt

60 ml/¼ cup extra-virgin olive oil, plus extra for drizzling

FOR THE TOPPING

100 g/scant ½ cup soft goat's cheese

100 g/scant ½ cup ricotta

6 fresh figs, cut into 5-mm/ ¼-inch slices

50 g/2 oz. blackberries (optional)

2 handfuls of rocket/arugula

2 tablespoons olive oil

1 tablespoon balsamic vinegar

1 tablespoon runny honey

sea salt and freshly ground black pepper

Makes 3

Combine the yeast and lukewarm water in a small bowl, stir to dissolve and set aside until foamy. Combine the flour, salt and olive oil in an electric mixer fitted with a dough hook. Add the yeast mixture and 150 ml/⅔ cup water and knead until well combined. Stand at room temperature, covered with a damp kitchen towel for about 1 hour, or until doubled in size.

Preheat the oven to 240°C (475°F) Gas 9.

Whip the soft goat's cheese with the ricotta and season well.

Turn the dough onto a bench and knock back, dusting lightly with flour, and bring mixture just together to form a smooth soft dough. Divide into three balls, then place on a lightly floured surface and cover with a lightly floured kitchen towel for about 20 minutes until doubled in size.

Put one of the balls of dough on a flour-dusted 22-cm/9-inch pizza tray and press outwards from the centre to flatten and stretch into a circle. Repeat with the other balls of dough. Drizzle with olive oil and bake in the preheated oven for 8 minutes.

Remove from the oven and spread the surface with the whipped cheese and top with the figs and blackberries, if using. Return to the oven for another 5–7 minutes. Take out of the oven and top with the rocket and drizzle with olive oil, balsamic vinegar and honey. Slice into small slices and serve.

Italian Flatbread with Tomatoes

This Italian flatbread has a simple topping of roasted cherry tomatoes, perfect as a pre-dinner nibble.

225 g/1¾ cups plain/all-purpose flour
1 teaspoon dried chilli flakes/
   hot red pepper flakes
1 teaspoon sea salt
150 ml/⅔ cup warm water
5 tablespoons olive oil, plus extra
   for brushing and drizzling
1½ teaspoons fast-action dried yeast
¼ teaspoon brown sugar
150 g/1 cup cherry tomatoes
3–4 rosemary sprigs
2 tablespoons dried basil
2 tablespoons dried parsley
sea salt and freshly ground
   black pepper

Serves 6

Mix the flour, chilli flakes/hot red pepper flakes and salt in a food processor. Put the warm water, 2 tablespoons oil, yeast and brown sugar in a jug/pitcher and add the liquid to the flour in a steady stream. Process for about 3 minutes until the dough forms a ball.

Transfer to a floured surface and knead for about 3 minutes. Transfer to an oiled bowl, cover and leave in a warm place until doubled in size.

Preheat the oven to 240°C (475°F) Gas 9.

Roll the dough into a long oval and prick all over with a fork. Mix together the tomatoes, rosemary and remaining 3 tablespoons oil. Brush the dough with oil, then top with the tomato mixture and season with salt and pepper.

Transfer to a baking sheet and bake in the preheated oven for 15 minutes, or until the dough is crisp. Sprinkle with the herbs and some salt and pepper, and drizzle with olive oil. Cut into small slices to serve.

Fig, Blue Cheese & Rocket Pizzette

Figs have a natural affinity with blue cheese, and the rocket/arugula balances the sweet and the salt with a peppery kick. Here the pizzette bases are smeared with a layer of Robiolino – a lovely soft, mild cheese not unlike cream cheese but with a slightly less pronounced flavour. Choose figs that are ripe, but not too soft. The savoury– sweet combination is a winner for accompanying a refreshing spritz.

300 g/10 oz. Robiolino (or other buttery cream cheese)
400 g/14 oz. Gorgonzola
4–5 ripe fresh figs
generous handful of rocket/arugula

FOR THE DOUGH
500 g/3¾ cups Italian '00' flour
10 g/2 teaspoons salt
5 g/1 teaspoon fresh yeast
250 ml/1 cup warm water

3 large baking sheets, floured

Makes 8

First, prepare the pizzette dough. Put the flour into a large mixing bowl and stir in the salt. In a separate bowl, stir the yeast and water together until the yeast has dissolved and then mix it into the flour. Bring everything together to form a soft dough. Leave the mixture to rest for 10 minutes, then lightly knead the dough, cover and leave to rest for 1 hour, somewhere not too warm.

Lightly knead the dough a second time and leave for a further 1 hour.

Knead the dough a third time, then cut into eight pieces. Roll the dough out into 20-cm/8-inch circles, making sure the bases are really thin. Lay them on the prepared baking sheets and leave for 30 minutes.

Meanwhile, preheat the oven to 240°C (475°F) Gas 9.

Spread the bases with a thin layer of Robiolino. Arrange small nuggets of Gorgonzola evenly over the top and bake for 8–10 minutes until the bases are crisp and golden.

Slice or quarter the fresh figs and arrange them over the pizzette. Garnish with rocket/arugula and serve immediately.

Tear 'n' Share 'Nduja Focaccia
with Basil & Preserved Lemon Dipping Oil

Here's something to impress and share with friends over drinks – it takes a little patience but is well worth the effort! Once pulled apart, each little bun has a soft fiery salami centre crying out to be dipped in the pungent bright green basil and preserved lemon oil.

1 recipe Basic Pizza Dough (page 110)
200 g/7 oz. 'nduja (spicy Calabrian sausage)
olive oil, for brushing
1 red and 1 green chilli/chile, thinly sliced into rings
1 teaspoon fennel seeds

FOR THE DIPPING OIL
50 g/2 oz. fresh basil leaves
4–5 tablespoons extra virgin olive oil
25 g/1 oz. chopped preserved lemon
dash of white wine vinegar (optional)
sea salt and freshly ground black pepper

shallow rectangular baking pan,
17 x 27 cm/7 x 10½ inches, lightly oiled

Makes 12 balls

Preheat the oven to 200°C (400°F) Gas 6.

Uncover the dough, punch out the air and divide it into 12 equal pieces. Pat or roll out each ball to a flat disk and place a teaspoon of 'nduja on the centre of each one. Bring up the edges over the 'nduja and pinch together in the centre. Flip over and arrange in the oiled pan. Repeat with the remaining dough and 'nduja – don't worry if the balls don't join up in the pan, they will when they have risen and proved. Cover loosely with oiled clingfilm/plastic wrap or a damp kitchen towel and leave to rise to the top of the pan for 30 minutes, or until doubled in size.

When risen, uncover and brush the tops with olive oil and lightly press in the chilli/chile rings. Scatter a few fennel seeds on top and bake for 35–45 minutes, or until golden.

Meanwhile, make the basil and preserved lemon oil by putting the basil and oil into a blender and whizzing until smooth. Mix with the chopped preserved lemon, taste and season, and add vinegar if necessary.

When the buns are cooked, leave to cool in the pan if you want them very soft, or turn them out onto a wire rack to cool if you like them drier. Serve warm with the dipping oil.

Potato & Olive Focaccia

Making a bread by mixing mashed potatoes with flour and anointing it lavishly with good olive oil is common all over Italy. It's best to use olives with the stones/pits in, as the pitted ones can dry out too much in the oven.

500 g/1 lb. 2 oz. baking potatoes, unpeeled

600 g/5¼ cups Italian '00' flour or plain/all-purpose flour, plus extra as necessary

½ teaspoon fine sea salt

25 g/1 cake compressed fresh yeast, 1 tablespoon/1 packet active dry yeast, or 2 teaspoons fast-action dried yeast

200 g/7 oz. large, juicy green olives, stones/pits in

150 ml/⅔ cup extra virgin olive oil

coarse sea salt

2 cake pans, 25 cm/10 inches and 4 cm/1½ inches deep or a large rectangular pan, lightly oiled

Makes 2 focaccias (25 cm/10 inches)

Boil or bake the potatoes in their skins and peel them while still warm. Mash them or pass them through a potato ricer.

Sift the flour with the fine salt into a large bowl and make a well in the centre. Crumble in the compressed yeast or add active dry yeast, if using. If using fast-action dried yeast, follow the manufacturer's instructions.

Add the potatoes and mix together with your hands until the dough comes together. Tip the dough out onto a floured surface, wash and dry your hands, and knead energetically for 10 minutes until smooth and elastic. The dough should be soft; if it isn't, add a couple of tablespoons warm water.

Divide the dough into two, shape each piece into a round ball on a lightly floured surface, and roll out into two 25-cm/ 10-inch circles or a large rectangle to fit whichever pan you are using. Put the dough in the pan, cover with clingfilm/ plastic wrap or a damp kitchen towel, and let rise for 2 hours.

Preheat the oven to 200°C (400°F) Gas 6.

Uncover the dough, scatter over the olives and, using your fingertips, make deep dimples all over the surface of the dough, pushing in some of the olives here and there. Drizzle with two-thirds of the olive oil, re-cover and let rise for another 30 minutes.

Uncover the dough, spray with water, and sprinkle generously with salt. Bake for 20–25 minutes until risen and golden brown. Brush or drizzle with the remaining olive oil then transfer to a wire rack to cool. Cut into small portions to serve.

Index

Amaretto Sour 41
Americano 37
anchovies: anchovy twists 58
  dried tomatoes, fresh anchovies & sizzled sage 68
  Gorgonzola & anchovy crostini 98
  'nduja & black olive tapenade mini pizzette 113
Aperol: La Passeggiata 17
  the Perfect Spritz 13
  Rosé Aperol Spritz 22
  Sparkling Aperitivo Punch 45
  Strawberry Rosé Spritzer 22
  Sunshine Negroni 33
arancini: blue cheese arancini 79
  Pecorino arancini with roasted cherry tomato sauce 80
  Pecorino, porcini & mozzarella arancini 77
  rosemary & Asiago arancini 76
artichokes: artichokes with prosciutto 68
  artichokes with Taleggio cheese & prosciutto 72
asparagus: egg & asparagus sandwiches 104
aubergines/eggplants: aubergine & tomato toothpicks 67
  aubergine, pesto, tomatoes & mozzarella rotolini 71

basil: basil & preserved lemon dipping oil 122
  fresh basil pesto 89
  Strawberry & Basil Bellini 46
beans: white bean & black olive crostini 102
Bello Marcello 38
bitter lemon: Porch-drinking Negroni 42
bourbon: Sparkling Manhattan 37
bread: bruschetta 108
  crostini 97–103
  focaccia 122, 125
  Italian flatbread with tomatoes 118
  mini sandwiches 107
  triangle sandwiches 104
breadsticks, peppered 59
bruschetta, grilled fig & prosciutto 108

Campari: Americano 37
  Classic Negroni 26
  Negroni Sbagliato 18
  the Negroni Cup 42
  the Perfect Spritz 13
  Porch-drinking Negroni 42

Sanguinello Fizz 25
capers: deep-fried sage leaves 57
  'nduja & black olive tapenade mini pizzette 113
  tuna, black olive, pine nut & caper crostini 103
  white bean & black olive crostini 102
Champagne: Sparkling Manhattan 37
cheese: artichokes with Taleggio cheese & prosciutto 72
  aubergine & tomato toothpicks 67
  aubergine, pesto, tomatoes & mozzarella rotolini 71
  blue cheese arancini 79
  courgette & Parmesan crocchette 83
  courgette, blue cheese & rocket rotolini 71
  deep-fried mozzarella sticks 87
  fig, blue cheese & rocket pizzette 121
  fresh fig, whipped goat's cheese, ricotta & rocket pizza 117
  Gorgonzola & anchovy crostini 98
  little cheese & ham toasties, Florian style 107
  little fried Neapolitan pizzas 110
  mozzarella pearls wrapped in prosciutto 63
  Parmesan crisps 57
  Parmesan fritters 52
  Pecorino arancini with roasted cherry tomato sauce 80
  Pecorino, porcini & mozzarella arancini 77
  pancetta & pecorino pizzette 114
  polenta fries with pesto 89
  speck & smoked ricotta crocchette 84
  puff pastry ricotta & spinach rolls 94
  roasted veg & mozzarella clubs 107
  Romano peppers, black olive paste & mozzarella rotolini 71
  rosemary & Asiago arancini 76
  speck & smoked ricotta crocchette 84
  thyme & Parmesan choux puffs 93
  Venetian cheese with sweet & sour onions 64
  wild mushroom & Parma ham tartlets 75
  see also ricotta
chickpea & rosemary fritters 55
chickpeas, rosemary roasted 64

chillies/chiles: chilli caramel nuts 52
  chilli jam 83
choux puffs, thyme & Parmesan 93
cipolline in agrodolce: Venetian cheese with sweet & sour onions 64
Cointreau: Bello Marcello 38
cornichons with salami 63
courgettes/zucchini: courgette & Parmesan crocchette 83
  courgette, blue cheese & rocket rotolini 71
crab mayonnaise & watercress sandwiches 104
crisps, Parmesan 57
crispy olive flatbreads 54
crocchette: courgette & Parmesan crocchette 83
  speck & smoked ricotta crocchette 84
crostini: Gorgonzola & anchovy crostini 98
  pea & mint crostini 97
  polenta crostini with caramelized fennel & prawns 101
  salt cod crostini 97
  tuna, black olive, pine nut & caper crostini 103
  white bean & black olive crostini 102
cucumber: Nonna's Garden 14

Dolin Bianco: Negroni Bianco Bergamotto 21
  Sunshine Negroni 33
Dubonnet: Tiziano 18

Earl Grey: Prosecco iced tea 30
egg & asparagus sandwiches 104
elderflower cordial: Hugo 14

fennel: polenta crostini with caramelized fennel & prawns 101
fennel seeds: pancetta & fennel puffs 90
figs: fig, blue cheese & rocket pizzette 121
  fresh fig, whipped goat's cheese, ricotta & rocket pizza 117
  grilled fig & prosciutto bruschetta with rocket 108
fish see anchovies; salt cod; tuna
flatbreads: Italian flatbread with tomatoes 118
  potato & olive focaccia 125
  tear 'n' share 'nduja focaccia 122
fries, polenta 89
fritters: chickpea & rosemary fritters 55

Parmesan fritters 52

gin: Classic Negroni 26
  High-Rise Martini 29
  La Passeggiata 17
  Negroni Bianco Bergamotto 21
  the Negroni Cup 42
  Newbie Negroni 26
  Porch-drinking Negroni 42
  Prosecco Iced Tea 30
  Sunshine Negroni 33
ginger wine: the Negroni Cup 42
grapefruit juice: La Passeggiata 17
  Sparkling Aperitivo Punch 45
grapefruit soda: Sunshine Negroni 33
grapes: Tiziano 18
grenadine: Sunshine Negroni 33

ham: little cheese & ham toasties, Florian style 107
  speck & smoked ricotta crocchette 84
  see also Parma ham
High-rise Martini 29
Hugo 14

iced tea, Prosecco 30
Italian flatbread with tomatoes 118
Italicus Rosolio di Bergamotto Liqueur: Negroni Bianco Bergamotto 21

La Passeggiata 17
lemonade: the Negroni Cup 42
lemons: Amaretto Sour 41
  polenta crostini with caramelized fennel & prawns 101
  Strawberry Rosé Spritzer 22
Limoncello: Prima Donna 41
  Sanguinello Fizz 25

Manhattan, Sparkling 37
Martini, High-rise 29
mint: Hugo 14
  Nonna's Garden 14
  pea & mint crostini 97
mushrooms: Pecorino, porcini & mozzarella arancini 77
  wild mushroom & Parma ham tartlets 75

'nduja: 'nduja & black olive tapenade mini pizzette 113
  tear 'n' share 'nduja focaccia 122
Neapolitan pizzas, little fried 110
Negroni: Classic Negroni 26
  Negroni Bianco Bergamotto 21
  the Negroni Cup 42
  Newbie Negroni 26
  Porch-drinking Negroni 42

Sunshine Negroni 33
Nonna's Garden 14
nuts, chilli caramel 52

olives: blue cheese arancini & griddled olives 79
crispy olive flatbreads 54
fried stuffed olives 60
'nduja & black olive tapenade mini pizzette 113
olive suppli with saffron salt 86
potato & olive focaccia 125
Romano peppers, black olive paste & mozzarella rotolini 71
tuna, black olive, pine nut & caper crostini 103
white bean & black olive crostini 102
orange juice: Newbie Negroni 26
Sanguinello Fizz 25
Sunshine Negroni 33

pancetta: pancetta & fennel puffs 90
pancetta & pecorino pizzette 114
panini, mini 107
Parma ham: artichokes with prosciutto 68
Parma ham, pear & rocket sandwiches 104
wild mushroom & Parma ham tartlets 75
passion fruit juice: Rosé Aperol Spritz 22
pea & mint crostini 97
peach purée: Classic Bellini 46
pears: Parma ham, pear & rocket sandwiches 104
Pear Bellini 46
peppered breadsticks 59
peppers: 'nduja & black olive tapenade mini pizzette 113
Romano peppers, black olive paste & mozzarella rotolini 71
the Perfect Spritz 13
pesto: aubergine, pesto, tomatoes & mozzarella rotolini 71
polenta fries with pesto 89
pine nuts: tuna, black olive, pine nut & caper crostini 103
pizza and pizza dough: anchovy twists 58
crispy olive flatbreads 54
fresh fig, whipped goat's cheese, ricotta & rocket pizza 117
little fried Neapolitan pizzas 111
Parmesan fritters 52
peppered breadsticks 59
tear 'n' share 'nduja focaccia 122
pizzette: fig, blue cheese & rocket

pizzette 121
'nduja & black olive tapenade mini pizzette 113
pancetta & pecorino pizzette 114
polenta: polenta crostini with caramelized fennel & prawns 101
polenta fries with pesto 89
rosemary & Asiago arancini 76
speck & smoked ricotta crocchette 84
pomegranate juice: Prima Donna 41
Tintoretto 33
Porch-drinking Negroni 42
porcini: Pecorino, porcini & mozzarella arancini 77
wild mushroom & Parma ham tartlets 75
potatoes: courgette & Parmesan crocchette 83
potato & olive focaccia 125
speck & smoked ricotta crocchette 84
prawns/shrimp, polenta crostini with caramelized fennel & 101
Prima Donna 41
prosciutto: artichokes with prosciutto 68
artichokes with Taleggio cheese & prosciutto 72
grilled fig & prosciutto bruschetta with rocket 108
mozzarella pearls wrapped in prosciutto 63
Prosecco: Bello Marcello 38
Classic Bellini 46
Hugo 14
La Passeggiata 17
Negroni Bianco Bergamotto 21
Negroni Sbagliato 18
Nonna's Garden 14
Pear Bellini 46
the Perfect Spritz 13
Prima Donna 41
Prosecco Iced Tea 30
Prosecco Mary 34
Rosé Aperol Spritz 22
Sanguinello Fizz 25
Strawberry & Basil Bellini 46
Tintoretto 33
Tiziano 18
puff pastry ricotta & spinach rolls 94
punch, Sparkling Aperitivo 45

radicchio, pickled 98
rice: blue cheese arancini 79
olive suppli with saffron salt 86
Pecorino arancini with roasted cherry tomato sauce 80
Pecorino, porcini & mozzarella arancini 77
rosemary & Asiago arancini 76

ricotta: fresh fig, whipped goat's cheese, ricotta & rocket pizza 117
Pecorino arancini with roasted cherry tomato sauce 80
puff pastry ricotta & spinach rolls 94
speck & smoked ricotta crocchette 84
rocket/arugula: courgette, blue cheese & rocket rotolini 71
fig, blue cheese & rocket pizzette 121
fresh fig, whipped goat's cheese, ricotta & rocket pizza 117
grilled fig & prosciutto bruschetta with rocket 108
Parma ham, pear & rocket sandwiches 104
Romano peppers, black olive paste & mozzarella rotolini 71
Rosé Aperol Spritz 22
rosé wine: Sparkling Aperitivo Punch 45
Strawberry Rosé Spritzer 22
rosemary: chickpea & rosemary fritters 55
rosemary & Asiago arancini 76
rosemary roasted chickpeas 64
rotolini, chargrilled vegetable 71

Sacred Rosehip Cup: Newbie Negroni 26
sage: deep-fried sage leaves 57
dried tomatoes, fresh anchovies & sizzled sage 68
salami, cornichons with 63
salt cod crostini 97
sandwiches, finger 104
Sanguinello Fizz 25
Sbagliato 18
semolina: tarelli 51
soda water: Americano 37
Newbie Negroni 26
Strawberry Rosé Spritzer 22
sparkling water: High-rise Martini 29
the Perfect Spritz 13
sparkling wine: Sparkling Manhattan 37
Sparkling Aperitivo Punch 45
speck: speck & smoked ricotta crocchette 84
spinach: puff pastry ricotta & spinach rolls 94
spritzes: the Perfect Spritz 13
Rosé Aperol Spritz 22
Strawberry Rosé Spritzer 22
strawberries: Porch-drinking Negroni 42
Strawberry & Basil Bellini 46
Strawberry Rosé Spritzer 22
Sunshine Negroni 33
suppli, olive 86

Suze: Negroni Bianco Bergamotto 21

tapenade: 'nduja & black olive tapenade mini pizzette 113
white bean & black olive crostini 102
tarelli 51
tartlets, wild mushroom & Parma ham 75
tea, Prosecco iced 30
tear 'n' share 'nduja focaccia 122
Tintoretto 33
Tiziano 18
toasties, little cheese & ham 107
tomato juice: Prosecco Mary 34
tomatoes: aubergine & tomato toothpicks 67
aubergine, pesto, tomatoes & mozzarella rotolini 71
chilli jam 83
dried tomatoes, fresh anchovies & sizzled sage 68
fried stuffed olives 60
griddled olives 79
Italian flatbread with tomatoes 118
'nduja & black olive tapenade mini pizzette 113
Pecorino arancini with roasted cherry tomato sauce 80
pizzette 114
tomato sauce 67
tramezzini misti 104
tuna, black olive, pine nut & caper crostini 103

vegetables: chargrilled vegetable rotolini 71
roasted veg & mozzarella clubs 107
vermouth: Americano 37
Classic Negroni 26
High-Rise Martini 29
the Negroni Cup 42
Negroni Sbagliato 18
Newbie Negroni 26
Porch-drinking Negroni 42
Sparkling Aperitivo Punch 45
Sparkling Manhattan 37
vodka: High-Rise Martini 29
Prima Donna 41
Prosecco Mary 34

watercress: crab mayonnaise & watercress sandwiches 104
whisky: Bello Marcello 38
white bean & black olive crostini 102
wild mushroom & Parma ham tartlets 75
wine: the Perfect Spritz 13
Strawberry Rosé Spritzer 22
see also Champagne; Prosecco; sparkling wine

Recipe Credits

Val Aikman-Smith
Italian flatbread with tomatoes
Olive suppli with saffron salt

Miranda Ballard
Cornichons wrapped in Salami
Mozzarella Pearls wrapped in Proscuitto
Pancetta, tomato & pecorino Pizzette

Julia Charles
Americano
Hugo
Rosé Aperol Spritz
Sparkling Aperitivo Punch
Strawberry Rosé Spritz

Maxine Clark
Anchovy twists
Deep-fried sage leaves
Grilled fig & prosciutto bruschetta with rocket
Little Fried Neapolitan pizzas
Nduja & black olive tapenade mini pizzette
Pancetta & fennel puffs
Parmesan crisps
Parmesan fritters
Peppered breadsticks
Potato & Olive focaccia
Sicilian chickpea & rosemary fritters (panelle)
Tear & share 'nduja foccaccia with basil & lemon dipping oil
Tuna, black olive, pine nut & caper crostini
White bean & black olive crostini

Ursula Ferrigno
Tarelli

Liz Franklin
Artichokes with prosciutto
Artichokes with taleggio cheese & prosciutto
Aubergine & tomato
Chargrilled vegetable rotolini
Chilli caramel nuts
Courgette & Parmesan crocchette
Dried tomatoes, fresh anchovies & sizzled sage
Fig, blue cheese & rocket pizzette
Fried stuffed olives
Gorgonzola & anchovy crostini
Little ham & cheese toasties Florian style
Roasted vegetable & mozzarella clubs
Mini panini
Pea & mint crostini
Salt cod crostini
Polenta crostini with caramelized fennel & shrimp
Polenta fries with pesto
Potato, speck & smoked ricotta crocchette
Ricotta & spinach rolls
Rosemary & asiago arancini
Rosemary roasted chickpeas
Venetian cheese with cipolline in agrodolce
Tintoretto
Tramezzini misti
Wild mushroom & Parma ham tartlets

Laura Gladwin
Bello Marcello
La Passeggiata
Negroni Sbagliato
Nonna's Garden
Prima Donna
Prosecco Iced Tea
Prosecco Mary
Sanguinello Fizz
Sparkling Manhattan
The Perfect Spritz
Tiziano

Carol Hilker
Deep-fried mozzarella sticks

Kathy Kordalis
Amaretto Sour
Blue cheese arancini & griddled olives
Fresh fig, whipped goats' cheese, ricotta & rocket pizza
Negroni Sbagliato
Pecorino arancini with roasted cherry tomato sauce
Thyme & Parmesan choux puffs

David T. Smith & Keli Rivers
Classic Negroni
High-Rise Martini
Negroni Bianco Bergamotto
Newbie Negroni
Porch-drinking Negroni
Sunshine Negroni
The Negroni Cup

Annie Rigg
Pecorino, porcini & mozzarella arancini

Photography Credits

Timothy Atkins
Pages 3, 10–11, 15, 16, 23, 24, 28, 32, 40, 48–49, 56, 62, 91, 95, 105.

Jan Baldwin
Page 50.

Gus Filgate
Page 108.

Mowie Kay
Pages 1, 2, 47, 152, 153, 61, 65, 66,70, 69, 73, 74, 78, 81, 82, 85, 88, 92, 96, 99, 100, 106, 112, 116, 120, 123, 124.

Erin Kunkel
Page 119.

Alex Luck
Pages 5, 6, 12, 17, 19, 20, 25, 27, 29, 30, 31, 34, 35, 36, 38, 39, 43, 44.

Steve Painter
Pages 53, 129.